The Good That Business Does

Robert G. Kennedy

Christian Social Thought Series

Number 9

Christian Social Thought Series, Number 9

ISBN 978-1-942503-32-3

Acton Institute
for the Study of Religion and Liberty

ACTON INSTITUTE

98 E. Fulton Street
Grand Rapids, Michigan 49503
Phone: 616-454-3080
Fax: 616-454-9454
www.acton.org

Printed in the United States of America

Contents

Foreword

There are perhaps more Christians in the field of business than in any other area of endeavor. That this is the case has nothing to do with a special compatibility between Christianity and business, of course; it is simply due to the fact that the broad category of business encompasses so many of the remunerative activities of contemporary life. Business is everywhere. It is only natural that Christians will be active participants.

Yet, as Robert Kennedy notes in this volume, Christian social thought has paid less attention to business than the prevalence of the latter would merit. Christian social thinkers have been especially negligent with respect to articulating the ways in which enterprise contributes to common and private goods: "the good that business does." Professor Kennedy, with experience in the business world and expertise in theology and management, begins to redress this deficiency in this, the first Christian Social Thought Series number of 2006.

Past topics in this series—justice, labor, immigration, corruption, and tort law—all touch on business. Business benefits from a stable rule of law, and it undermines its own prosperity when it neglects law through participating in corrupt practices. It is similarly hurt by a culture of litigation that stifles entrepreneurship and risk-taking, yet it contributes to such a culture when it produces items that are harmful or operates in legally or morally problematic ways. Business relies on skilled and dependable labor; indeed, a business in many respects *is* its employees. By treating its employees, its customers, and other businesses justly, business contributes to the common good.

Professor Kennedy deals with these and other moral obligations of business and toward business in this volume. In the process, he helps to elucidate the place of the modern business enterprise within contemporary society. In the best tradition of Christian social thought, his starting points are what we know about morality through reason and revelation and what we know about business through empirical observation. Using this method, he articulates the responsibilities of business in a way that is both realistic and in keeping with the timeless truths of the moral law.

Among Professor Kennedy's investigations is the current debate about the "social responsibility" of business, which he engages in a unique and insightful fashion. Business's social obligations, it turns out, are both more and less than what many contemporaries believe.

Businesspeople are not immune to sin, and Professor Kennedy does not pretend that all businesses live up to his model at all times. What he presents is, admittedly, an ideal, but it is an ideal that many businesses approach in their day-to-day activities. In other words, Christian social thought offers a standard to which men and women in business can and should aspire—and the standard is sometimes more fully, sometimes more poorly, upheld by the many and diverse individuals who comprise the innumerable companies that populate the world's economic landscape. The challenge is not fundamentally different from that confronted by every Christian in living his or her vocation.

Kevin Schmiesing
Acton Institute

1 Introduction

This book is about the good that business does. More precisely, it is a reflection, in the light of the Christian social tradition, on the legitimate role that business plays in modern life and its critical contribution to the common good of the communities in which we live.

Though we do not often think of it this way, one of the major political challenges of the modern era has been to manage the integration of business into the structure and life of the civil community. This challenge had its beginnings in premodern Europe as commerce and trade revived in the late Middle Ages. It became more urgent with the European discovery of the New World and spread across the continents on the sails and wings of the Industrial Revolution. Today, when we speak of the "new" challenges of globalization, we are really addressing an old problem that has taken on worldwide dimensions.

While trade is as old as human communities, business (understood as a system of organizing work and trade, which comes to include stable companies and formal markets) is a

The author would like to thank Kevin Schmiesing for his patient and insightful editing of this volume and the author's colleague Michael Naughton for the many fruitful conversations they have had on these topics.

child of civilization. In its early manifestations in the ancient world, it was largely personal (that is, individual merchants rather than companies) and dealt with goods that were not produced locally. The merchant was a kind of transport agent, who bought in one place and sold in another. Farmers and craftsmen sold their goods and services to their neighbors more or less directly. Great fortunes, by and large, depended upon the ownership of land, not on commercial success. There were customs and laws, to be sure, but nothing so systematic as we know today.

Banks and other trading organizations developed in the late Middle Ages, but it was the first stirrings of truly global trade in the fifteenth and sixteenth centuries that provoked the development of a genuine system of business. This in turn posed new challenges to the political and religious structures of the day. Business activities generated (or at least accumulated) a great deal of wealth and, in doing so, spanned national and even continental boundaries. Along with wealth came power and influence that could and did rival those possessed by kings and princes but that resisted political control. How can a trading organization be controlled, for example, whose headquarters might be in London, Amsterdam, or Madrid but whose operating decisions are made in Calcutta, Jakarta, or Mexico City?

The continuing expansion of the business system not only challenged individual rulers but also, eventually, political structures. As others have observed, there seems to be an important connection between a systematic market economy and democratic forms of government.[1] In the absence of artificial barriers, a business system does not respect nobility or social status; it does respect cleverness and energy and determination. Where business flourished—perhaps as a con-

---

[1] See Michael Novak, *The Spirit of Democratic Capitalism* (New York: Simon and Schuster, 1982).

dition for business to flourish—governments became less monarchical and more democratic.

Cultural challenges appeared as well. Given the growth of systematic economic activity in Spain and Italy, the Catholic Church was compelled to review its thinking about usury and other business practices. Although they are little remembered today, a cadre of brilliant Spanish theologians in the sixteenth and seventeenth centuries thought deeply about the new economic realities.[2] Their work laid some of the foundations for the modern discipline of economics.[3]

By the nineteenth century, with the Industrial Revolution well under way in England and Germany, the challenges posed by business to politics and culture were acute. Ancient patterns of life, rooted in the land and traditional crafts, in aristocracy and the Church, were disrupted in a generation. New technologies, new forms of organizing work, and new ways of employing wealth were powerful agents of permanent change.

Many of the changes brought mixed results. On the one hand, manufactured goods (and other things) became available to a large population who before could never have afforded them. On the other hand, a great many in Europe were able to escape the crushing servitude of rural life only to enter a new sort of servitude in industrial towns and cities. The vulnerable in the old order were often also vulnerable in the new order, but what protections existed in rural society often disappeared in the factories and the mines.

---

[2] See Alejandro A. Chafuen, *Faith and Liberty: The Economic Thought of the Late Scholastics* (Lanham, Md.: Lexington Books, 2003) and Juan Antonio Widow, "The Economic Teachings of Spanish Scholastics," in *Hispanic Philosophy in the Age of Discovery*, ed. Kevin White, Studies in Philosophy and the History of Philosophy, no. 29 (Washington, D.C.: Catholic University of America Press, 1997), 130–44.

[3] See Joseph Schumpeter, *The History of Economic Analysis* (New York: Oxford University Press, 1954).

Because the new business system was so disruptive and unpredictable, there was a natural desire to manage and control it, whether for the sake of those who were swept into it or for the sake of those who wished to preserve their positions of status and power. Attempts to manage the business system could take the shape of socialism (in one of its forms), various regulatory systems, or perhaps the harnessing of political and cultural energies to hold back the tide in favor of more primitive economic structures.[4]

In the end, of course, none of these attempts has been fully successful, and some have been spectacular and costly failures. These failures have not had the effect of discouraging those who would tame the business system—in many cases it has not even persuaded them to adopt different tactics—and so the challenge remains.

What also remains among the public is a certain distrust of business, particularly of large corporations. We are apprehensive about the power they have to affect the lives of great numbers of people and often concerned that they will not use this power well. This distrust is not relieved by the failure of business leaders (to say nothing of economists and other thinkers about business) to explain how they understand business to be integrated within the social order.[5]

---

[4] *Globalization* is a fluid term, but we might understand it to mean (at least) the expansion of the modern business system throughout the world. The same sorts of problems that arose with the emergence of the business system in Europe and North America are now confronting the less developed countries of the world who must not only manage the internal challenges their own communities face but also contend with the competition offered by developed economies. History suggests that however much they might want to do so, it is not possible to resist the business system and achieve relative prosperity.

[5] Nor is it mitigated by the occasional dramatic misbehavior of the managers and executives responsible for major companies. For an entire generation, company names such as Enron, Tyco, Worldcom, and Parmalat will conjure up images of businesses run amok.

It is just this question—about the integration of business within a healthy social order—to which this book is addressed.

Economics, law, and other social sciences have contributed greatly to our understanding of the business system and its functioning. They have done less well in helping us to understand the role that business plays in society and how business and society ought to interact. The purpose of this volume is to consider how the Christian social tradition, with special emphasis on its manifestation in Catholic social teaching, might shed new light on this old problem.

To pursue this inquiry, we need to be clear about what, in general, economics and law have to tell us about the nature of the business system. We will also need to assemble some of the key elements of Christian social thought in order to construct a sound theory of business and society. With this in mind, it will be helpful to consider briefly how the Christian tradition has approached business, and so this will be our starting point.

II   A Brief History of Christian Thinking About Business

Although Christian theology is properly centered on the life and teaching of Jesus, it is still heir both to the Jewish religious tradition and to secular culture and philosophy. Early Christian thinking about business mimics the attitudes and ambivalence of these two traditions, and thus there is some value in understanding how these roots have shaped it.

One Root of Christian Thinking: The Jewish Tradition

The Jewish tradition, partly evidenced in the Old Testament, respected prosperity as a sign of God's favor, yet also saw wealth as a temptation to distraction from one's obligations to God and neighbor. The people of Israel were time and again seduced from observance of the Law by prosperity and physical contentment. They forgot that their true strength lay in God's faithfulness to his covenant and not in material possessions. God's response when they strayed, as foreshadowed and explained by the prophets, was to withdraw his protection and expose Israel and Judea to their enemies. Their wealth, such as it was, was never proof against the power of Assyria or Babylon. Only when the people returned to faithful observance of their covenant duties, and God restored his protection, did they reestablish the foundation of their prosperity. Only then did they remember that all wealth is a gift from God and not a substitute for his friendship.

As a consequence, in Jewish thought, the wise man is not necessarily someone who renounces wealth, but someone who understands its proper role in human life.[6] Like Job, he respects and enjoys material possessions, but he never forgets that friendship with God, not wealth, status, or power, is the defining element of human life. The fool misunderstands this. The fool believes that wealth may replace God in one way or another and places its pursuit and protection at the center of his life.[7] Thus Jewish tradition, to which the first Christians were heirs, regarded wealth (and therefore also commerce) with some worry and suspicion.

The early Christian community, as noted in Acts, apparently held what property it had in common.[8] Some have concluded that this should be taken as a model for later Christian communities and that it is evidence of a fundamental Christian hostility toward private property. However, this view is probably not correct. Other New Testament passages reinforce the Jewish view that wealth could be an obstacle to establishing one's relationship with God and enjoin that wealth be used well. While there is some criticism of the means by which wealth was sometimes acquired, the possession of wealth itself is not condemned.

Throughout the Wisdom literature of the Old Testament, men are advised to fear the Lord and remain faithful, to be industrious (for the sake of their basic needs), and to

---

[6] See Sirach 31.8–11. Note that in general throughout the Wisdom literature of the Old Testament, the wise and the just are contrasted with the fool and the wicked. The wise man understands the true nature of the world and acknowledges God's sovereignty; as a result, he is committed to justice. The fool, consumed by his own desires and inclinations, turns easily to wickedness.

[7] See Psalms 14.1, 49, 52; Proverbs 11.28, 28.25–26; Sirach 5.1–10, 31.1–7.

[8] Acts 2.44–45.

recognize that prosperity is a gift of the Lord.[9] The teachings of Christ and the apostles as related in the gospels and epistles affirm this approach to wealth: the acquisition of property is accepted, but inordinate attachment to possessions ("love of money") is condemned.

Another Root: The View of Business in Greek Thought

Beginning with the second generation of the Christian community, as faith in Christ moved beyond the Jewish nation to the Greco-Roman world, Christians encountered two realities. The first was the richness and complexity of a world marked by relative peace and stability, which provided a foundation for widespread trade. The second was Greek philosophy.

The two towering figures of the Greek philosophical tradition were Plato and Aristotle, who were both from wealthy families and suspicious of the merchant class. In the *Republic*, where Plato describes his vision of the ideal society, merchants and traders are a lower class of citizen ("of little use for any other purpose") and given a limited role.[10] In his later book, the *Laws*, he recognizes the value of their work, but he also considers such work to be corrupting. As a result, he prohibits citizens from engaging in it, directly or indirectly, and reserves it strictly for foreigners.[11]

Similarly, Aristotle, no enemy of wealth as such, distinguishes two modes of life, one concerned with the acquisition of sufficient property to make a good life possible for a household (*oikonomia*) and the other with the acquisition of not property but money (*chrematismos*).[12] *Oikonomia* is naturally limited to the needs of a family and is the foundation

---

[9] Sirach 11.10–28 is an extended example of a typical sentiment.
[10] Plato, *The Republic*, 2.371d
[11] Plato, *The Laws*, 11.919
[12] Aristotle, *Politics*, 1.8–9.

of a prosperous society. In this mode of life, when sufficient property is accumulated for the family, in principle, energies that were once directed to acquiring property can be turned to the leisure activities of a free man: philosophy, aesthetics, participation in civic duties, and so forth.

Chrematismos, by contrast, leads to an accumulation of money without limit, and for that very reason it is irrational. The person pursuing this mode of life, if he really is seeking ever more money (and not, say, the power or fame or admiration that money can bring), is attempting to possess more than he can ever use. In doing so, he forgoes other activities and goals (nurturing friendships, for example) for the sake of something that can bring him no net benefit.

Oikonomia is the appropriate occupation of a citizen, while *chrematismos* is regarded as unworthy of a free man and a citizen. Both Plato and Aristotle consider a life devoted to the unlimited accumulation of money (which they understand to be a tool) to be debased because the value of a tool is always in its use, not in its mere possession. No reasonable person seeks to acquire tools without regard to the goals that the tools permit us to achieve.

The key to understanding their hostility to commercial activity, therefore, lies in their assumption (explained at length by Aristotle) that merchants genuinely do aim at the acquisition of money without limit.[13]

One may reasonably argue that Plato, Aristotle, and their disciples had too constrained a view of economic life. Modern scholarship reveals that the economic life of the ancient world was far more sophisticated than the descriptions of the philosophers would lead us to believe.[14] Furthermore, far from being true *chrematistikoi*, there is good reason to believe

---

[13] Aristotle, *Politics*, 1.9.

[14] See, for example, Humfrey Michel, *The Economics of Ancient Greece* (New York: Macmillan, 1940) and M. I. Finley, *The Ancient Economy* (Berkeley: University of California Press, 1973).

that many merchants aimed simply to acquire sufficient wealth to purchase the requirements of a household and retire to a life of agriculture and *oikonomia*. Still, the caricature of the grasping, insatiable merchant is a common one throughout history, even if it is only occasionally accurate. Plato and Aristotle did not create the caricature, but they assumed its truth, and their views were enormously influential in shaping the attitudes of the secular culture into which the early church emerged.

The larger world of the early Christians was the world of the *pax Romana*, the peace of Rome. It was a world in which travel was relatively easy and safe, as evidenced by the missionary journeys of the apostle Paul. It was also a world made safe for commerce, and so trade flourished. During these years, and well into the Middle Ages, it is safe to say that when philosophers and theologians wrote about business they had traders and merchants in mind, not farmers and craftsmen. The archetypal businessman was a merchant.

This led to certain conceptual difficulties because the work of the merchant was insufficiently valued. While the labor of the farmer or the craftsman clearly changed the land or the material on which he worked, the labor of the merchant usually produced no real change in his merchandise. His contribution was transporting products from one place to another and charging what he could at his destination. Furthermore, the merchant's stock in trade was usually not a necessity. Food, clothing, and shelter were the products of permanent members of the community: farmers and craftsmen. By contrast, the merchant was frequently gone from his community and often dealt in comparative luxuries. Such factors—rootlessness, poorly understood contribution, the nature of the merchandise—probably contributed to the fact that the merchant was frequently held in low esteem in the ancient world.

Foundations of the Modern Era

Some twenty-five years after Columbus came ashore in the Caribbean, Martin Luther issued his formal challenge to the Catholic Church. These two events are illustrations of the two great challenges facing the Church in the period following the Middle Ages. The external challenge was to evangelize a brand new world (including sub-Saharan Africa, India, and the Far East, which were all known to the medieval world but largely inaccessible before sea travel). The internal challenge was to preserve the integrity of Christendom. Sadly, in contrast with its success in the Middle Ages, in this period, the Church failed dramatically in addressing both challenges. The close association of Catholic missionary activity with the brutalities of conquest and colonialism limited the success of evangelization, and the Reformation permanently divided Christianity in the West.[15]

Nevertheless, despite its diminished influence in society, the Church did take action and developed an important voice on matters of commerce. The discovery of the Americas as well as the Reformation provoked bishops to institute far-reaching reforms and prompted theologians to develop an extensive body of analysis and doctrine in moral theology, a significant portion of which concerned the practice of business and political economy.

The starting point for the theologians' analysis was pastoral. As trade became a larger part of life, bishops and pastors were more frequently confronting issues in the confessional and in public life involving moral questions about

---

[15] To be sure, Christianity took deep root in the New World, though it was not able to influence political and economic structures as well as it might have done. The success of evangelization in Asia was quite limited, in part because of the strong religious traditions in China and India. As for Africa, it is hard to escape the conclusion that missionary work was too closely associated with colonial activities to permit it great success.

business affairs.[16] The theologians, especially the Spanish scholastics of the sixteenth and seventeenth centuries, framed elaborate and insightful responses. In doing so, they assumed that Catholic businessmen genuinely wished to be guided by their analysis (just as, perhaps, Catholic doctors looked to theologians for moral guidance in the early twentieth century).

They recognized that the world of commerce was not exclusively a Catholic, or even a Christian, world, and so they situated their discussions in the context of treatises on justice. By and large, then, the requirements of morality for business were understood to be the requirements of the virtue of justice and not the principles of the gospel (though justice is hardly in conflict with the gospel). These theologians also acknowledged the legitimacy of commerce and its vital role in providing goods for the community and in increasing the nation's wealth. The honest merchant, in their view, carried on God's work by distributing fairly the resources that the Creator had scattered unevenly about the earth. Commerce, as a result, was an instrument of justice and a vehicle for improving the fellowship of the human race.

Moreover, they built upon, and considerably expanded, medieval discussions of profit, recognizing the value of the contributions of merchants and businessmen in making goods and services available even when they did not alter what they sold. Their careful and detailed analysis of the

---

[16] The issue of usury has been investigated at great length by a number of authors. See, for example, John T. Noonan, *The Scholastic Analysis of Usury* (Cambridge, Mass.: Harvard University Press, 1957). It played a prominent role in early economic analysis by the theologians because they confronted the need to reconcile the traditional concept of the nature of money with a wide variety of novel business practices. They soon realized that the concept of money that underlay the prohibition of usury was inadequate to describe the real uses of money in a sophisticated economy. This led them to analyze more deeply other aspects of commerce to determine their moral character.

legitimate grounds for profits would be quite familiar to a modern economist. In contrast with modern economic theory, however, they also reaffirmed the traditional opposition to seeking profit for its own sake. Their justification of profit always, in one way or another, depended upon showing that it was fair compensation. They made no attempt to justify the activity of the merchant who sought gain without limit, nor could they do so within the framework of Christian theology.

A critical element, however, that was not sufficiently emphasized by the theologians (and poorly understood outside the Church as well) was the possibility of creating wealth. The economy of the Middle Ages was relatively stagnant and based upon the land. Wages and prices might vary little over a century. In such circumstances, it was easy to assume that the total wealth of a society, like the land it occupied, was a fixed amount. One could accumulate wealth only by acquiring it in some way from others, who would thereby have less. The just distribution of money and property was consequently of paramount importance.

Until the eighteenth century, business and trade, the businessman and the merchant, were virtually synonymous. The latter half of the eighteenth century saw the development of a new form of business: manufacturing on a large scale. As this and other forms of industrialization developed in the following century, they posed yet another challenge to moral theology. In one sense, though, the issues were similar to those addressed so forcefully more than a millennium earlier by bishops such as Ambrose and Chrysostom, who were dismayed at the existence of extreme poverty alongside great wealth.[17] In another way, however, the Industrial Revolu-

---

[17] Texts from Ambrose, Chrysostom, and a number of other patristic authors can be found in Charles Avila, *Ownership: Early Christian Teaching* (Maryknoll, N.Y.: Orbis Books, 1983) and Peter C. Phan, *Social Thought*, Message of the Fathers of the Church, no. 20 (Wilmington, Del.: Michael Glazier, 1984).

tion taught a lesson that many in the Church did not adequately understand: that wealth can be created and that the business system is not a zero-sum game.

The emergence of large-scale enterprises, whether in manufacturing, transportation, communications, retailing, or any other field, concentrated the control (if not the actual ownership) of productive resources in the hands of a small number of businessmen. These men not only possessed great wealth, but they also controlled jobs, goods, and services for many people. Like the wealthy of the ancient world, these men, in the view of moral theologians, had serious responsibilities not only toward the poor, but also toward all those who depended upon them (e.g., employees and customers). The inadequate discharge of these responsibilities may be said to have provoked both socialism as a political force as well as the emergence of Christian economic thought as a distinct body of doctrine.

In sum, as the Western world moved into the nineteenth century, the thinking of the Catholic Church about business was still encumbered to a significant degree by the narrow traditions of earlier millennia. The insights and sophistication of some early modern theologians had a limited influence on this thinking. In the end, the Church continued to regard business activities as likely to be tainted with greed and remained insensitive to the revolutionary possibilities of wealth creation. As a consequence, the Church has not adequately supported businesspeople in the pursuit of their occupation nor has it been able to exercise much influence to shape the interaction of business and society.

In order to do both, Catholic social thinking must develop a deeper understanding of the nature of business and its contribution to the common good.

III   What Economics and the Law Have to Teach Us About Business

One of the principal objectives of this small book is to present a view deriving from the Christian social tradition of what business could be if it fulfilled its potential. It therefore has a normative goal, of a sort, that is to encourage people who are engaged in the management of businesses to think somewhat differently about how they ought to do their work (and to encourage those outside business to recognize and support the good that business does). In pursuing this goal, however, the intention is not to repudiate but to complement the two other disciplines that study the nature of business: economics and law.

No attempt to bring the Christian tradition to bear on the question of business and the common good can ignore the contributions and influence of economics and law. On the one hand, economics is irreplaceable as the foundation for an understanding of the way in which people make choices, while law sets in place the rules for the commercial arena and shapes our understanding of its relationships and institutions.

On the other hand, we must be clear about the character and limits of what these two disciplines have to teach. Each begins with certain assumptions, and these assumptions shape the observations and conclusions they offer. Neither claims to offer answers to ultimate questions about human nature or human goods. Both are deeply informed by the experience of human behavior.

For its part, the Christian tradition also claims vast experience of human behavior, but it adds to this some claims about the meaning and purpose of human life. Before we move on to consider in greater detail key concepts from the social tradition, it will be worthwhile to reflect briefly on what we learn and do not learn from economics and law.

The Contribution of Economics to Our Understanding of Business

While the theologians of the sixteenth century made some pioneering efforts to understand economic activities in the new, more complicated world brought into being by the European discovery of the Americas, economics as a formal discipline is not rooted in their work.[18] Instead, economics is a modern *social* science, given birth by the turn away from the theological worldview that marked the Enlightenment of the eighteenth century. By and large, the early economists were deliberately engaged in a project quite different from the project of the theologians. Where the theologians were eager to understand economic activities in order make clear the requirements of justice, the early economists (many of whom were also moral philosophers) were interested in the study of economic activities for other reasons.

This is not to say that the economists had no concern for justice but rather that their principal practical goal was to

---

[18] We should acknowledge from the beginning that economics, while resembling the physical sciences in some ways, is by no means as unified and coherent in its basic principles. Like philosophers, economists often differ sharply in their judgments about fundamental concepts, exhibiting disagreements far deeper than any one might expect to find in, say, physics or chemistry. Therefore, the remarks that follow about economics are not intended to characterize every economist but rather to speak to the general shape of the discipline.

study economic behavior in order to improve it, that is, to make it more efficient and effective. In pursuing this goal, they set aside the theologians' convictions about ultimate goods and ends for human persons (about which we will have more to say later). They concentrated instead on explaining the way in which people *actually* made choices about production, trade, and consumption rather than deliberating about the choices people *ought* to make. The result was a growing emphasis on the observation and measurement of economic behavior and a diminishing concern with its moral implications.

This general tendency has led some people to conclude that economics is not only dreary but also morally insensitive. Neither criticism is fair. As a social science, economics by design sets aside most questions of morality as outside the scope and competence of the discipline. To be sure, there are many moral questions related to economic policies and behaviors, but it is not the task of economics to address these questions, nor does the discipline possess independent resources for resolving them.[19] It rightly turns these over to theology and moral philosophy. Its contribution to the larger picture is to improve our understanding of the patterns of human behavior, without which the practical application of moral principles becomes highly problematic.

As a consequence, economics is not, strictly speaking, a normative discipline.[20] It does, however, have something to say about the choices people ought to make and the preferences they ought to have. It does this, though, only on the

[19] Note Pope John Paul II's remark in the 1991 encyclical *Centesimus annus*, no. 44: "Of itself, an economic system does not possess criteria for correctly distinguishing new and higher forms of satisfying human needs from artificial new needs which hinder the formation of a mature personality."

[20] A normative discipline is one that tries to identify, or prescribe, what courses of action people ought to choose in order to be morally upright. The principal normative disciplines are ethics and moral theology.

assumption that certain goals or objectives are sought or preferred.[21] Its directives are *hypothetical* imperatives.

Following Kant, modern moral philosophers often distinguish between hypothetical imperatives (commands) and categorical imperatives. The distinction is roughly this. A categorical imperative is a moral principle binding on all persons. For example, prohibitions against murder, theft, and fraud apply to everyone, and anyone who wishes to be a morally upright person (as we should all aspire to be) must abide by them.

A hypothetical imperative, instead, assumes a particular goal and identifies the behaviors necessary to achieve that goal. A simple example of a hypothetical imperative would be directions to a destination. Not everyone wants to travel from New York to Washington, but *if* you do wish to do this, then you must head south. The question of *why* someone would want to go to Washington—there could be morally good and morally bad reasons—is irrelevant. On the assumption that a person wants to make the trip, there are certain things that must be done.[22] For its part, because it deals largely with hypothetical imperatives, economics can identify the means that someone must choose to accomplish chosen goals efficiently and effectively without addressing the questions of whether those goals, or the necessary means themselves, are morally sound. This additional judgment, which of course ought to be made, depends upon another discipline, such as philosophy or theology.

---

[21] Rational choice theory, a fundamental assumption of economics, contends that individuals make deliberate choices aimed at achieving their objectives most efficiently and effectively, but it remains entirely agnostic about which objectives individual persons *ought* to pursue.

[22] It does not matter that there might be a number of ways to achieve the goal (e.g., drive a car, ride a train, take an airplane, pedal a bicycle). Each means would involve *hypothetical* rather than *categorical* imperatives.

Nevertheless, economics is not entirely value free. In many of its forms, it takes its beginnings from a set of assumptions that can give a moral color to the discipline as a whole. There are three such assumptions that we ought to keep in mind as we consider the relationship of business and the common good.

The first assumption is that the proper focus of economics is the person, the autonomous individual seeking to maximize his or her satisfactions and faced with choices in a world populated with competing individuals seeking to maximize their satisfactions. While economists recognize that individual persons live and seek their satisfactions within a society, only these individual satisfactions are considered. The common good tends as a result to be considered a set of conditions, or accommodations, under which the autonomous individual is able to seek whatever satisfactions he or she chooses with maximal efficiency and minimal interference from others. One consequence of this, apart from the thin notion of the common good, is that it is difficult in economic theory to account for, or even to recognize, goods that are shared by their very nature.

For example, true friendship (not merely a friendship of utility) is a good enjoyed through participation. It is a good that one enjoys by contributing to and participating in the activity of friendship, not by taking something away from the relationship. Economics tends to reduce human goods to those things obtainable by work or transaction and therefore to miss a wider range of goods. An implication for business is that goods of participation that might be an important part of a good and healthy organization are systematically overlooked.

A second assumption, as mentioned above, is that there are no criteria available for determining the worthiness of the ends for which individuals act. Human objectives simply are what they are. Some objectives ought to be discouraged by law or custom on instrumental grounds because the actions required to achieve them (for example, murder, theft, fraud, and so on) significantly interfere with others' pursuit of their objectives. However, this is merely a relative evaluation, and economics must remain silent on all questions of permanent, authentic value.

This can lead to a common view in marketing that managers have no standing to make independent judgments about the moral quality of the products or services their companies offer to the public. To be sure, companies should not offer products that are against the law to offer, that provoke disobedience to the law, or that offend the values of the community. Beyond that, however, they should refrain from withholding products or services that customers want merely on the grounds that the managers think them unworthy.[23]

The third assumption concerns the goods that satisfy human needs and wants. Economics focuses principally, if not exclusively, on human needs and wants that are satisfied by scarce goods.[24] Embedded in this assumption is the conviction that human satisfactions are material, or at least that the principal wants we desire to satisfy are for material things. Furthermore, human wants are assumed to be limitless, which contributes to making material goods scarce.

---

[23] Organizations or individual merchants, in this view, could legitimately choose not to offer a product or service on moral grounds, but in doing so they cannot appeal to universal moral principles but instead are simply maximizing their individual satisfactions.

[24] Human beings have material needs and desires (for food, clothing, golf clubs, cell phones, iPods, and so on) as well as immaterial needs and desires (for love, friendship, knowledge, and so on). Most material goods are limited in principle and tend therefore to be scarce (though not always and everywhere). Immaterial goods, on the other hand, are not quantified and therefore do not diminish in the way that material goods can be exhausted. Sharing knowledge, for example, does not mean that less is available for others. The focus of economics is upon material goods, which are characterized by scarcity rather than abundance. Some economists, to be sure, have attempted to extend economic patterns of analysis to categories of immaterial goods but with mixed success.

Several corollaries follow from all this. One is the inference that competition is inevitable if human wants are not adjusted. Because the goods that satisfy human persons are scarce, the normal mode of pursuit of these goods must be competitive.[25] It is not surprising that economics often sees human interactions and relationships in this mode, but we ought to guard against seeing all business relationships as competitions.[26]

Another inference is that the human desires and wants that can be satisfied through work, especially through work in a business setting, are all for scarce material goods. In other words, the goods that business provides to shareholders, employees, customers, communities, and others are entirely material. While it is legitimate for economics to focus on such goods and the discipline makes no systematic claim that all human goods are scarce and material, it is all too easy for people to lose sight of the wider range of human goods.

By contrast, the Christian social tradition adopts three different starting points, as we shall see. This tradition sees the person as essentially social, not radically individual. It also insists that there are authentic goods that fulfill genuine human needs. Our desires are not the measure of our needs, but, in fact, we may indeed desire things that are truly bad

---

[25] When there is not enough to go around to satisfy everyone's wants, the distribution of scarce goods must entail either competition or compromise (where some or all receive less than they desire) or both. Compromise is often the result of a desire to avoid the costs of competition and not often enough the consequence of a commitment to justice. Human associations that approximate real communities—think of a functional family—as opposed to loose collaborations tend to work hard to diminish competition. Some economists have also attempted to explain the actions of individuals in a community in terms of negotiation and competition rather than genuine collaboration but once again with mixed results.

[26] The tendency to exaggerate the competitive elements of business is widely in evidence. This is one reason that there are so many sports and military metaphors in use in management, marketing, and finance.

for us. Finally, the tradition claims that there is a much wider range of goods for human persons. Certainly, some of these goods are scarce and material but the most important goods, the ones that most truly fulfill us as persons, are not. These different starting points lead us in a new direction in regard to business and the common good.

The Contribution of Law to Our Understanding of Business

Legal theory is far older than economics, but like economics it depends upon concepts of the human person that it rarely examines carefully.[27] It also has a practical orientation.[28] Once again, like economics, law is concerned with efficiency, but it also must aim at maintaining harmony in the civil community, and it can aspire to justice. In the contemporary Anglo-American legal world, the underlying view of the person has become pluralistic, and several incompatible concepts of the person now compete to shape legal theory and ultimately the legal structures that govern everyday lives.

Many of these competing views do not directly affect business but instead will have considerable influence in areas such as medicine and family law.[29] Others have already shaped

---

[27] We will understand *law* here to encompass laws and rules created by legislative bodies and regulatory agencies as well as judicial decisions.

[28] An excellent discussion of the law and economics movement and its relationship to the Catholic social tradition can be found in Steven Bainbridge, "Law and Economics: An Apologia" in *Christian Perspectives on Legal Thought*, ed. Michael McConnell, Robert G. Cochran, Jr., and Angela Carmella (New Haven, Conn.: Yale University Press, 2001), 208–23. I would take issue with some of Bainbridge's analysis, but his discussion of economics and legal theory is clear and seems quite right.

[29] Recent movements in legal theory, some of which have influenced fundamental legislation and Supreme Court decisions, have tended to affirm the radical autonomy of the individual. One implication of this tendency that is pertinent to our discussion is the conviction that the older notion of a nature

the law concerning product liability and employment. Our immediate concern, though, is with the legal view of the nature of a business and its relationship to the community. There are two ideas that are important here.

The first assumption is the conviction that a business is to be operated principally, though perhaps not exclusively, for the benefit of the owners or shareholders. This question was famously tested in a lawsuit brought by the Dodge brothers against Henry Ford.[30] The Dodges had been early investors in the Ford Motor Company but after a few years became dissatisfied with the dividends the company was paying. They argued that as shareholders they deserved a much larger share in the company's spectacular profitability. Henry Ford contested this and argued that he was using the profits of the company to "employ still more men; to spread the benefits of this industrial system to the greatest possible number, to help them build up their lives and their homes." In other words, Ford claimed that he paid a fair dividend and that surplus resources were better and more properly used to improve the lives of workers and expand the business. The Michigan Supreme Court decided in favor of the plaintiffs, holding that the directors of a corporation cannot operate the company merely for the "incidental benefit" of the shareholders. Ford was ordered to pay a huge dividend to his shareholders.

---

shared by all human persons must give way to a positivist notion of individual human choosing, where what the individual chooses is good simply because he chooses it. This moves beyond the agnosticism of economics with regard to the ends that are truly good for people to pursue, to a commitment to protect the liberty of individuals to choose as they wish even when their choices may undermine communities. To the extent that this view is generally adopted and shapes legislation and judicial decisions, it becomes more difficult to argue, for example, that businesses have a duty to the community to produce goods and services that address authentic human needs and not merely wants.

[30] *Dodge v Ford Motor Co.*, Supreme Court of Michigan, 1919. 204 Mich. 459, 170 N.W. 668.

The implication for business, particularly for public corporations, is that directors, and by extension all of the executives and managers of a company, must attend primarily to the interests of the owners and shareholders. In the absence of other indications, this interest is presumed to be the maximization of the wealth of the shareholders, which is most easily measured by the value of the stock. No claim in law is made that companies must be operated exclusively for the benefit of the owners but there is a presumption that decisions should favor them.[31] In practice, this often means that managers focus intensely on creating value for shareholders and overlook negative impacts on employees, customers, and civil communities.

Clearly, the law conceives of a business not as a community but as a piece of valuable property to be owned and exploited. Customers, civil communities, suppliers, creditors, and employees in particular are not part of the business but stand outside it. The contributions of these parties to the operation of the business are obtained by transaction and exchange. The obligations of the business to them are no more than to fulfill the terms of the exchange and to avoid unnecessary harms. Given such a foundation, it becomes difficult to justify a positive obligation on the part of business to the common good.

The second assumption, however, is that while businesses may not have an obligation to attend in positive ways to the common good of the civil communities in which they exist and function, they may be free to do so. One version of this

---

[31] As additional evidence of the plurality in legal theory, we might look to the widespread legislation in the 1980s that sought to create barriers to corporate takeovers. This legislation gave permission to directors to resist purchase offers if the directors thought that the new owners would make decisions damaging to employees, customers, communities, and others. This suggested without asserting too strongly that companies were not always to be operated primarily for the benefit of the shareholders.

view would hold that all contributions to the common good should be justifiable in terms of subsequent benefits to the business. For example, a local business that sponsors a softball team should be able to justify this on the basis of the advertising and good will its sponsorship generates, which should translate later into increased sales. Similarly, the actions of a public corporation to sponsor, say, an athletic or cultural event, must either be justified in terms of business advantages or the consent of the shareholders.

Contributing to the common good of the civil community, therefore, is something that a business may do, but the law does not conceive it to be something that a business ought to do as a consequence of what it is.

As we shall see, the Christian tradition offers a more expansive understanding of what a business is and of the goods it serves. In doing so, it offers not so much an opposing view as a corrective to the visions provided by economics and law.

IV An Overview of the Catholic Social Tradition

Catholic social teaching (CST) is an element of a broader moral tradition. As such, it should be understood not as a static body of doctrine, passively received by one generation after another, but rather as a dynamic body of knowledge—not unlike the physical sciences—that is augmented and developed in linear fashion over time. To put it another way, CST is not a codified body of principles and rules for arranging social interactions but is rather an evolving response to a concern about the context in which human persons grow, develop, and live their lives—a natural result of the Catholic understanding of the human being as an embodied spirit and a social creature.[32]

Contrary to a common view, this tradition did not originate with the modern papal encyclicals that have contributed to it. In its various manifestations, it is as old as the Church itself, being well represented in the writings of the patristic period (the first centuries), the Middle Ages, and the early modern period.[33]

---

[32] See Pope John Paul II, *Sollicitudo rei socialis* (1987), no. 1.

[33] *Compendium of the Social Doctrine of the Church* (Vatican City: Libreria Editrice Vaticana, 2004), no. 72. This document is an essential summary of the Catholic social tradition.

CST has generally had *two modes*, or functions, though one or the other has often been especially emphasized in different times and places. One mode is a *critique* of aspects of social life insofar as they influence the well-being of human persons (and perhaps insofar as they can be influenced).[34] The second mode is a *set of proposals* concerning the shape and substance of a society that would fully respect human dignity.[35] More crudely put, in one mode, CST identifies what is wrong with a society, while in the other, it attempts to describe what a good society should be.

Furthermore, there are *three dimensions*, or areas of attention, that are integral to CST. One dimension is *political*, where the tradition considers forms of government, jurisprudence, and the proper uses of power. A second dimension is *economic*, where the tradition considers questions of human needs and scarce resources. The third dimension is *cultural*, where the tradition pays attention to the richness of social arrangements, artistic expressions, and other manifestations of human intelligence and creativity that shape and give an identity to members of a community. Once again, different dimensions have been emphasized at different times. The political dimension, for example, was of greater concern in

---

[34] The writing and preaching of the early Church fathers, prior to the acceptance of Christianity under Constantine, was only mildly critical of political and economic conditions, partly out of concern that Christians not be seen as threats to the established order and persecuted. Beginning in the fourth century, as Christians moved into positions of authority and society became at least nominally Christian, leading bishops of the fourth century, such as Ambrose, Basil, and Chrysostom, were severely critical of the social conditions of the time. In particular, they strenuously exhorted wealthy Christians to care for the poor.

[35] By the time of the early Middle Ages, when Europe was being shaped into Christendom, representative thinkers turned their attention to the responsibilities of princes who cared for their people. Charlemagne became the type of the good Christian king (and a model of sorts for Tolkien), and later writers, such as Aquinas in the thirteenth century and Bellarmine in the sixteenth, wrote about the nature of a good society.

medieval Europe than the economic dimension, while today the opposite is true. These dimensions, too, can be explored at different levels. For example, papal contributions on economic topics in the late nineteenth and early twentieth centuries tended to focus on local and national economic matters, such as the tension between labor and ownership, while later contributions gave more attention to economic relationships between nations.

It must also be emphasized that this tradition is not by any means the exclusive province of the hierarchy of the Church. The Church's self-understanding is that it is the particular responsibility of the laity to bring the gospel to the secular world—to the home, to the school, to the workplace, to the political arena—and so CST especially profits from the contributions of lay thinkers and practitioners.[36] The popes and bishops ordinarily conceive their role to be to articulate principles and encourage sound applications. What the laity require from bishops, pastors, and other teachers is clarity about the enduring insights of Christian faith, not detailed plans of action.[37] In other words, the laity need principles, not

---

[36] This theme is a constant in Church documents of the past forty years. See, for example, the Second Vatican Council (1962–65): *Dogmatic Constitution on the Church* (*Lumen gentium*), no. 36; *Pastoral Constitution on the Church in the Modern World* (*Gaudium et spes*), no. 43; and *Decree on the Apostolate of the Laity* (*Apostolicam actuositatem*), no. 2 and *passim*. This theme also receives considerable emphasis in Pope John Paul II's 1988 postsynodal apostolic exhortation, *The Vocation and Mission of the Lay Faithful* (*Christifideles laici*).

[37] Nevertheless, in recent years, and in some countries more than others, bishops and their staffs have been relatively aggressive in commending specific pieces of legislation or in supporting certain public policies. While bishops as individual citizens are surely free to express their views on public matters, the practice of official advocacy has occasioned considerable discussion within the Catholic community, and some concern that this constitutes an intrusion on the part of the bishops, or their staffs, into a properly lay arena. Some Catholic legislators have expressed their frustration with episcopal representatives who have presented a particular political preference as a matter of Catholic doctrine, thereby compromising Catholic legislators who, as a matter of prudential judgment, support alternate policies.

prescriptions. If the principles are clear, the laity can, and will, devise a variety of applications to real-world problems.

It may be fairly said that all of Catholic moral theology is an unfinished project. While fundamental principles may be preserved, the understanding of the implications of principles may always be deepened, and new challenges call for new applications. This is particularly true for CST for two reasons. First, human societies are unstable. Political structures change, cultures mutate, and new forms of economic organization are devised. All of this calls for continual reflection and adaptation. Second, despite two millennia of development, the tradition has not systematically examined every aspect of human social life. For example, as noted earlier, there has been a bias in the tradition against a careful reflection on the importance of creating wealth (and not merely distributing it), and so there has been little contemporary reflection on the topic.[38] A similar limitation exists concerning the function, structure, and management of business organizations.[39] The tradition has devoted considerable attention to families and to civil societies but has not caught up with

---

[38] This may be changing, but the suspicion of wealth is deeply embedded in Catholicism. Furthermore, the very age and diversity of the tradition makes it difficult to grasp it as a comprehensive whole. The work of a number of sixteenth-century Spanish theologians, for example, who produced some very sophisticated analyses of the problems of wealth and commerce, has been largely forgotten and still remains virtually inaccessible to English-speaking readers. The access in English to their work that does exist has been provided by Marjorie Grice-Hutchinson, *Early Economic Thought in Spain* (Boston: G Allen and Unwin, 1978); Alejandro A. Chafuen, *Faith and Liberty: The Economic Thought of the Late Scholastics* (Lanham, Md.: Lexington Books, 2003), and the *Journal of Markets & Morality*.

[39] We may even go so far as to say that CST has hardly moved beyond the critical mode in its treatment of wealth creation and business. The combination of apprehension about the temptations of wealth and a deeply rooted sympathy for labor has moved most thinkers in this field, including many bishops, to do little more than scold businesspeople for their attitudes and practices. This, too, is changing, but the constructive mode of CST in this area is still seriously underdeveloped.

the modern proliferation of intermediate associations or with the peculiar problems they present. (We will address this issue in the next chapter.)

As a consequence, it will be necessary to reconstruct an analysis of the business system upon the foundational principles of CST.

We should, therefore, be clear about three of the critical foundational principles of the tradition.

The Reality of God's Merciful Love

The foundation of the entire social tradition is the *reality of God's merciful love*. The love that God has for us—who are utterly undeserving of that love—is the model of the love that we ought to have for one another. This contrasts starkly with the wisdom of the world that tells us that we are all in competition with one another and that to receive our friendship and help people must first be deserving of it. For this reason, reducing Catholic social teaching to "social justice" or speaking of "social justice" as *the* objective of Christian action in the world can be misleading. Not every undesirable situation is a result of deliberate injustice. Given the fallen human condition, a just world can also be a harsh and unforgiving world because justice gives to us what we merit, not necessarily what we need. Instead, while Christians ought to seek justice, they must not be content with this but must always be willing to go beyond justice to mercy. As one moralist has said, "Mercy is the justice of the Kingdom."[40]

The reality of God's love also reminds us that everything we possess—our property, our talents, our skills, our resources—is a gift from God. These gifts are conditional, and the condition attached to them is that they be used for God's purposes. One of these purposes is that we ourselves be

---

[40] See Germain Grisez, *The Way of the Lord Jesus*, vol 1, *Christian Moral Principles* (Chicago: Franciscan Herald Press, 1983), 212–14.

brought to a share in his life through the use of these gifts. This ordinarily means that our use of the gifts may be (and should be) personally rewarding, both spiritually and materially, but it also means more. While we have the right, and indeed the duty, to care for ourselves and our families, we have a more fundamental duty to discover what God wishes us to do with what we have been given. In other words, each person must discern his vocation and pursue it courageously and wholeheartedly.

The Nature of the Human Person

The second key idea concerns *the nature of the human person*. Pope John Paul II has said in his encyclical *Centesimus annus* that "the guiding principle of ... all of the Church's social doctrine is a correct view of the human person."[41] This correct view is rooted in the first chapter of Genesis, which insists that human persons alone are made in the "image and likeness" of the Creator. The Second Vatican Council took up this theme when it insisted that human beings are the only creatures that God made for their own sake, and not to serve some further purpose in the created order.[42] Three conclusions follow from this.

The first is that every human person, no matter what his age or condition, possesses an irreducible value, or worth, or dignity that absolutely must be respected. This dignity can never be deliberately stripped away to serve another purpose, no matter how important.

The second implication is that human persons most properly image the Creator in possessing the Godlike capacities to reason and to choose freely. All human activities and structures must respect the ability of the individual to think (and must not, for example, merely manipulate people through

---

[41] *Centesimus annus*, no. 11.

[42] *The Pastoral Constitution on the Church in the Modern World* (*Gaudium et spes*), no. 24.

their emotions) and to exercise his freedom (and so must not dominate people by a misuse of power).

Furthermore, it belongs to human dignity for people to exercise their freedom well, to take responsibility for their actions, and to provide for their own material welfare and that of their families through their work.[43] It is disrespectful of the dignity of the person to make a competent individual, or a group of people, simply dependent upon others for the necessities of life. Instead, authentic human dignity requires that conditions be created and nurtured that permit people to care for themselves. Welfare structures, however well intended, that have the effect of trapping people in dependent relationships, do not fully respect human dignity. At the other extreme, structures that prevent people from participating fully in the economic and political dimensions of social life (e.g., unjust distributions of land and productive property, artificial barriers to entry, and so forth[44]) also fail to respect human dignity.

The third implication is that human persons, in their very nature, also reflect the reality of God as a community, as a Trinity. In other words, just as God exists in the intimate communion of Father, Son, and Spirit, so, too, are human persons social at the core of their being. Men and women form communities and societies of all sorts, not merely because it is efficient to do so (though this may also be true) but because life in community is one of the deepest expressions of their likeness to the Creator.

---

[43] See *Compendium*, nos. 287, 294.

[44] An example of a barrier to entry is unreasonable licensing requirements (such as for hairdressers and taxi drivers), which effectively prevent potential competitors (often lower income, aspiring entrepreneurs) from operating businesses. For an argument concerning the way minimum wage laws act as barriers to employment, see John Barry, Samuel Gregg and Michel Therrien, *A Living Wage: Lessons in Economic Justice*, (Grand Rapids, Mich.: Acton Institute, 2001).

Each of these implications profoundly shapes the Christian vision of human life and human communities.

Justice and Property

The third basic idea has to do with *justice and property*. Justice is the broader concept. The possession and use of property must always be judged in the light of the principles of justice, but justice concerns more than property. Justice at its most fundamental concerns what each person, as an image and likeness of the Creator, deserves to have. It characterizes our relationships with others when we live with them in peace and harmony and when we have done what we can and should do to ensure that they have everything they need and deserve, as human persons.[45] It characterizes each of us as persons—we possess it as a virtue—when we are deeply and firmly committed to give others what they deserve.

The Catholic moral tradition has long distinguished three dimensions of justice. One is commonly called commutative, or exchange, justice, which concerns the relationships of individuals or groups to one another. A sale, for example, is just if each party receives something of roughly equal value from the exchange; someone who has damaged another's property has a duty of commutative justice to repair that damage.

A second dimension is distributive justice, which concerns fairly parceling out benefits and responsibilities with respect to common possessions. This requires that persons who are alike be treated in the same way but permits (or even requires) that persons who are different in relevant ways be treated differently.

---

[45] Underpinning the Christian notion of justice in practice is the conviction that God has provided an abundance of material goods and resources to the human family. The challenge is to use human ingenuity, shaped and motivated by charity and justice, to insure that every person is able to have access to his fair share of this abundance. That material poverty and deprivation continue to exist is a sign of sinfulness, not scarcity.

For example, in distributing dessert after dinner, parents in a family ordinarily have a duty to give each child an equal share because there are usually no relevant differences between the children. On the other hand, the same parents rightly give a dose of medicine only to the children who are ill. Similarly, on the level of the society, it may be quite fair for the government to extend greater benefits to persons who are disabled and to require higher taxes from persons with greater wealth.[46]

The third dimension of justice is what the tradition has often called general justice. This refers to the general obligations that individual members of a community have to the common good of that community. Thus, for example, children have a duty in justice to help with household chores, adults have a duty to pay taxes, and everyone has a duty in his own way to contribute to the common good of each community to which he belongs.

In his 1931 encyclical, *Quadragesimo anno*, Pope Pius XI referred to *social justice* and so introduced the term to Catholic discussions.[47] The term is ambiguous and we may understand it in two ways. First, it is sometimes used substantively to refer to the condition of a society. We will have achieved social justice when a society is well-ordered, that is, when burdens and benefits are fairly distributed and the

---

[46] This discussion concerns the consistency of such policies with justice. It should be noted that legislators must carefully consider all the potential consequences of their policy choices, including the long-term economic effect of the incentives and disincentives that are created. For example, tax policies that impose progressively higher marginal rates are intended to distribute the burden of supporting government more fairly by collecting more from those who have more. This can have the unintended consequence, however, of discouraging additional job creation and wealth creation. Flat tax systems that collect more from those with higher incomes without discouraging their additional economic activity, can also be constructed.

[47] For an examination of the Church's use of the term *social justice*, see Stephen J. Grabill, et al., *Doing Justice to Justice* (Grand Rapids, Mich.: Acton Institute, 2002).

dignity of each individual is properly respected. On the other hand, social justice can be considered a virtue of individual persons. In this case, it generally means a commitment on the part of the individual to work in every way possible to support the common good. More recently, following Pope John Paul II, we have come to call this solidarity.[48]

What role does property play in all this? Each person deserves to have property and indeed requires it for his fulfillment. CST vigorously defends the right of individuals to own property of all sorts but insists that this right is not absolute. No one has a right to excess food, regardless of how legitimately he acquired it, when others around him are starving. At the same time, charity obligates us to use our resources to meet the real needs of our families and neighbors before we address the needs of others far more remote.

Property can take many forms: land, physical objects, money and capital, and ideas. Whatever its form, it is ultimately a gift from God and an instrument intended to promote genuine human fulfillment. Property in all its forms is one component sustaining the richest and most fulfilling life for every human person. CST is not committed to a dreary, subsistence view of human life, but rather to a life of abundance, where property never becomes an end in itself but always serves authentic human fulfillment.

The rightful possession and use of property are governed by the principles of justice in all three of its forms. Individuals and groups must always be fair in their transactions with others. Where common resources or common responsibilities are concerned, persons must be treated in the same way unless there are relevant differences. Finally, individuals must always be prepared to use their property to support the common good.[49]

---

[48] *Sollicitudo rei socialis*, nos. 38–40.

[49] In the twentieth century, concerns and questions about the right use of property have tended to crowd out other issues within the Catholic social tradition.

The Catholic social tradition, of course, is larger and richer than these three principles. They do, nevertheless, provide a foundation upon which we can attempt to construct a modern theory of the business system and its relationship to civil society. To do that we need to examine and to adapt several further concepts related to CST, and it is to that project that we now turn.

V Business and the Common Good

What is the good that business does? Any organization or any system deserves to be called good only to the extent that its activities serve human well-being. Individual business organizations, as well as the whole modern system of business (with its extensive infrastructure), will therefore be good to the degree that they address authentic human needs for individuals and provide support for the common good of the civil community. To integrate business within this larger community, whether we consider this on the local, national, or global levels, requires that we explain the good that business does. The next step in shaping a modern theory of business rooted in the Christian social tradition, then, is to consider the concepts of authentic human needs and common goods and to relate these ideas to the nature of a business organization.[50] We will begin by examining briefly the question of what might be the goods that genuinely fulfill human persons.

---

[50] We need to remember that the theory we are constructing is not descriptive (as are economic and legal theories of business) but aspirational. That is, it is not another attempt to describe how businesses actually behave but rather an effort to offer a vision of what businesses could and should be in society if they were to fulfill their potential to contribute to human well-being.

What Do People Really Need?

Any goal that human beings can pursue is, in the language of moral philosophy, a "good." Indeed, one of the fundamental moral insights of Western philosophy is that people always strive for what they believe to be good. No one can consciously and deliberately aim at something that he thinks is bad. The person contemplating suicide, for example, is not focused on the badness of death but on the good of a release from pain. People can, however, be mistaken about the goodness of a goal or the goodness of a means to achieve that goal. We can even want what in fact may not be good for us to have. Goals, like investments, are objectively good or bad. They do not become good because we aim at them nor does our desire for them make them good. Instead, we need to think about the possible goals that are available to us and to make wise choices about which ones to pursue.

The challenge of distinguishing real goods from illusory goods is a critical one and faces us in both our private and professional lives. We can respond more effectively to that challenge by coming to a clearer understanding of the categories of goods that truly fulfill human beings. We can call these *basic goods*.

When we consider the seemingly limitless array of goals that people pursue and the countless ways in which they structure their lives, we can understand why some people think that there are no goals essential to human happiness and well-being. Some people pursue wealth, while others care very little for it. Some people want children and family, while others delight in their solitude. Christian moral philosophy is committed to the idea that human beings all share a common nature, which, in fact, makes them human. As a result, it is possible to identify some very general goods that every human being naturally strives to include in his or her life.

This last point is an important one because it helps us to avoid a common criticism of any attempt to ground ethics in human nature. The complaint is that an ethics grounded in nature would conclude that only one sort of life is really worth living (presumably the one lived by the ethicist) and that other sorts of lives, or lifestyles, are wrong. This is a serious misunderstanding of the idea of human nature. In fact, a better understanding of human nature can help to explain why good human lives can take an almost infinite variety of forms.

The analogy of a healthy diet and good cooking might help us to understand this better. Suppose we say that everyone needs a certain amount of calcium in his or her diet. Without it there are some serious health consequences. This does not mean that everyone must drink milk, though milk can be an excellent source of calcium. A number of other sources could work just as well, and the actual amount needed by individuals can vary from person to person and from one time of life to another. The need for calcium in some form from some source, however, is grounded in biochemistry and the nature of the human animal. We might even say that there is a "law" of calcium for human beings. No government enforces it; there are no criminal penalties for violating it, but there are consequences that follow from ignoring the law.

Basic human goods are like the calcium in a diet, to say nothing of the protein, vitamins, minerals, carbohydrates, and other substances that the human body needs to remain healthy. A human life also needs a range of goods to be truly happy and fulfilling. Like the elements of a healthy diet, a person will not normally die without one or another of the human goods, but her life will be less happy and satisfying than it might have been. A life without some of the basic goods is still a human life and perhaps even an admirable one in many ways. Although we have a remarkable capacity to settle for less than we might have had in our lives, we should not call that compromise complete happiness or the best life possible.

Another point needs to be made as well. For any goal that we pursue, a question can reasonably be raised about why we are seeking that particular goal. There are two kinds of answers we can give because there are two very general kinds of goals. We pursue some goals because they are useful, or instrumental, for some other goal. For example, someone might say that his goal is to buy ice cream at the grocery store, and this might really be the purpose of a series of actions (putting gas in the car, driving to the store, getting cash out of the ATM, and so on). The successful purchase of the ice cream is the reason for doing everything else, but is it the final reason? In fact, the final goal—the last goal in a series of coordinated actions—might be to enjoy a dish of ice cream that evening with a friend. Every other action is taken in pursuit of that goal. Every goal we pursue is either pursued (or valued) for the sake of some further goal, or it is pursued (or valued) simply for itself. The first kind are *instrumental* goals (or goods), while the second are *final* goals (or goods).

Basic goods, then, are goods that are fulfilling for human beings in an irreducible way; they are final goods. They are valued for what they are, never for their usefulness in bringing us to other goods (which, of course, would then be even more basic). The categories of basic goods we want to discuss are the rock bottom of human motivations and pursuits, and they will give us a general description of what every business must seek to serve in some way.

A great deal of work has been done by philosophers in recent decades to refine our understanding of the notion of basic goods.[51] For our purposes, we will identify basic goods

---

[51] In this section, I am drawing upon and adapting the work of Germain Grisez and John Finnis, both of whom have written extensively on this subject over a period of several decades. Grisez's principal work here is *The Way of the Lord Jesus*, vol. 1, *Christian Moral Principles* (Chicago: Franciscan Herald Press, 1983). Finnis's principal work is *Natural Law and Natural Rights* (Oxford: Oxford University Press, 1980).

in six categories: life and health, beauty, truth, action, harmony, and friendship. A genuinely good human life will include instances of goods in each category, just as a good diet includes items from each of several basic food groups. Again, like a diet, there is no common scale for measuring the value of items in one basic group against the value of items in another. If calcium is really needed for health, then no amount of protein or Vitamin C can substitute. In the same way, goods in the category of beauty cannot be measured in any meaningful way against goods in the category of truth.

In their operations, business organizations have the potential to satisfy genuine human needs by making the basic goods real in specific ways. They may do this internally through the conditions they create for employees or externally through the products, services, and other goods they offer to their customers and communities. To make this a bit clearer, we will consider each of the basic goods in turn.[52]

> **Life and Health.** The basic good of life includes life itself and also whatever relates directly to biological life, including health, safety, and the avoidance of pain. Like all of the basic goods, life is something that we can and should wish for others as well as ourselves. In a business context, goods related to life and health are pursued and respected internally when management insures that the workplace is as free as possible from hazards, that the work is not physically harmful, that the equipment and the furniture used do not contribute to long-term injuries, and so forth. These goods can be pursued externally

---

[52] There are actually countless ways in which businesses might pursue and respect the basic goods. The examples offered in the following paragraphs are meant to be illustrative, not exhaustive. It should be noted, too, that some businesses are particularly focused on products or services related to one of the basic goods. Examples would include industries or fields such as healthcare, fashion, or sports.

through products and services that protect life and restore health, through efforts to make products safer to use and by adopting production methods that diminish pollution and health hazards for the general community.

This good is neglected or damaged when an organization puts too much pressure on employees (causing stress-related illness), tolerates unsafe working conditions or product defects, and commits or omits any number of other activities that undermine the health and reasonable comfort of employees, customers, and the community.

Beauty. The basic good of beauty involves the experience and appreciation of beauty, order, and harmony in the world outside of the individual person. This beauty may be found in another person, in the world of nature, in the arts, in sports, and in many other contexts. A business pursues and respects goods related to beauty internally in any number of ways. It does so, for example, when it works to keep the workplace clean, when it builds and decorates tastefully (as distinct from merely building and decorating expensively). It also does so when it permits and encourages individuals in the organization to decorate their work areas themselves, for beauty may take many forms and appeal to widely differing personal tastes. Externally, a business pursues this good when its products, for example, are not merely functional but aesthetically pleasing as well. This good is neglected or damaged by a preference for functionality without elegance and a tolerance of ugliness, disorder, and filth.

In this context, it is important to note the real distinction between what is necessary and what is luxurious. Beauty, or aesthetic experience, is truly necessary for human flourishing. A life without beauty is stunted and poor. The absence of beauty does not kill the body, but it can kill the spirit. The necessities of life include more than those things without which a person dies; they include everything that makes a human life full and satisfying. Luxury, on the other hand, is always an embellishment that adds little or nothing to the human good involved. Luxurious products and services consume resources without serving a real human need.[53]

Action. From the toddler's demand that she be allowed to do it herself to the retired person's determination to remain busy, human beings demonstrate the value they place on activity over passivity. The basic good of action includes all activities done for their own sake (as opposed to activity undertaken and valued only for the sake of something else). Action of this sort is ordinarily skillful performance of some sort, whether play or work, whether done clumsily or excellently well.[54] Thus, a person is pursuing the basic good of action in playing golf, even if she is only beginning and does not yet play well.

The key idea is that it is action in which the person values the acting independently of whatever benefits that activity might produce. For this reason, the sort of activity that realizes this basic good is more often playful than productive. Even productive activity (that is, work), however, may fall into this category to the extent that the activity itself can be valued by the person quite apart from the value

---

[53] The words *luxury* and *luxurious* are overused. They are really not synonyms for excellence but when used properly convey a sense of wasteful excess.

[54] In the Catholic tradition, following the work of Pope John Paul II (see his 1981 encyclical, *Laborem exercens*) play may be broadly considered to be any activity done simply for the sake of the enjoyment of performing the action. It need not be limited to games. Work, on the other hand, is always productive activity (or at least activity that aims at producing something) and therefore activity valued principally because of what results from it.

attached to whatever is produced.[55] An example might be the work of putting in a garden. Some people relish the tasks involved and consider the flowers or the vegetables to be an added bonus.

The good of action is most fully realized by someone who can perform an action at a level of excellence. In a business context, management pursues and respects goods related to action internally when it permits and encourages employees to enjoy and take pride in their work and when it makes training and evaluation available so that employees may perform in ways that are more humanly satisfying. A business does this externally when its products and services (sports equipment or instruction, for example) help others to engage in action for its own sake. This good is neglected or damaged when too much emphasis is placed on productivity to the exclusion of pride and quality, or when workers are required unnecessarily to follow a fixed prescription for a job that permits them little or no personal satisfaction.

Truth. The basic good of truth is accurate knowledge of any subject where the knowledge is valued for its own sake, that is, where it is knowledge that satisfies curiosity rather than knowledge that is useful.[56] It may include knowledge about the atomic structure of carbon, or the history of the Civil War, or the behavior of African beetles. Like goods in the category of action, goods in the category of truth can

---

[55] Many goods in this category have a sort of mixed character, where the activity involved is not only productive of other goods but also valued in itself. For example, someone might play tennis to get exercise or lose weight and at the same time simply enjoy the very playing of the game, independently of any other benefits the play might bring.

[56] This is a philosopher's distinction that should not distract us here. Useful knowledge, while often very valuable and worthwhile, is nevertheless valued only for what it can produce or obtain, and therefore cannot be a *basic* good (though what the useful knowledge might allow us to obtain could be a basic good).

have a mixed character. We might value a piece of knowledge both for its own sake and because we can do something with it. Only the knowledge, however, that we value for its own sake is a basic good.

In the context of business, goods related to truth are pursued and respected internally when employees are given opportunities for enrichment apart from increasing their productivity. (Once again, productivity is not a bad thing, but it is valued for the sake of something else and so cannot be a basic good.) They are pursued externally through journalism and education as well as through the creation of a number of products and services, from structuring tours of exotic locations to making documentary films and publishing on history.

This good is neglected or damaged whenever knowledge is made defective through misrepresentation, manipulation, or deliberate lying, as well as, at times, through deception or concealment.

Harmony. Every human being experiences not only a life of interactions with other persons and things but also an interior life. Part of the experience of that interior life is the experience of conflict between incompatible desires and inner pressures or between thought and action. Quieting these conflicts is a matter of personal maturity (which is not the same thing as age). The mature person acquires a degree of harmony between conflicting emotions and desires, and learns how to calm the inner tension we all sometimes feel. She also aligns her actions with her thinking so that her actions become practically reasonable, in harmony with her knowledge of reality and her judgment about what is best to do. This is not an easy achievement. It depends upon self-control, which here means bringing one's emotions and desires under the control of reason. (This does not mean that reasonable people cannot be passionate people, but just that reasonable people are not overwhelmed by their passions.) It also requires clear thinking about the real world.

In a business context, we pursue and respect goods related to harmony when we avoid imposing the sorts of pressures that create inner conflicts for people, whether employees, customers, clients, or others. Contrarily, we can perversely create these conflicts by offering opposing incentives (do we work for sales or for safety?), by mistreating employees or customers (creating a temptation to steal), by underpaying suppliers, and so on. Managers also respect goods related to harmony in the workplace when they model and recognize unbiased, reasonable decision-making. An organization plagued by bureaucratic politics, for example, is one in which employees must develop coping mechanisms that are often unreasonable.

Friendship. The basic good of friendship involves harmony not within the person but between the individual and other persons. We often have a much more narrow concept of friendship, which involves a special sort of relationship, and one that we usually cannot maintain with more than a few people at a time. The more general sense intended here is the sort we have in mind when we say that we want to be on good terms with the world. No healthy person wants enemies. We often take it as a sign of maturity that a person is able to create and maintain good relationships with everyone with whom they come in contact. The good of friendship entails peace and justice between people and organizations (to say nothing of nations).

In order to pursue and respect the good of friendship internally in a business, managers do not need to aim at creating affection but rather to ensure that employees (and customers, suppliers, creditors, and so on) are treated justly. This good is also respected, for example, when employees are encouraged to collaborate with one another to achieve organizational goals, when an atmosphere of caring concern for members of the organization is deliberately sustained, and when loyalty is evident. Friendship is neglected or damaged by excessive politics, by rumors, by wasteful personal competition, and in many other ways.

It should be clear from this description of the basic goods that one action or situation can often integrate two or more of them with one another. For example, a healthy workplace can also be a beautiful one, or skillful performance can also enhance friendships.

An appreciation of the basic goods can support sound decision-making in business by providing a touchstone against which to measure alternatives. While decisions that clearly harm instances of the basic goods directly must be rejected, it is rarely the case that only one course of action is legitimate and defensible. The preferred alternative should be the one that best respects one or more of the basic goods, which are after all the ultimate reasons we have for making decisions and acting.

For their part, managers must be clear about the ways in which their organizations can and do create instances of basic goods for people, both inside the organization (employees) and outside (customers and communities). Organizations do not have a responsibility to pursue every good imaginable for the people who cooperate with them, but they must, at minimum, avoid harming basic goods. In the most fundamental way, organizations are superior to the extent that they are able to pursue and respect more instances of the basic goods more deeply.

Common Goods

Because human persons are naturally social beings, and their genuine fulfillment inevitably involves a community of some sort, common goods are of critical importance. Attempts to understand and resolve issues of justice in a community must sooner or later deal with the question of what it means for goods to be common (as opposed to private). Unfortunately, the term *common good* is quite equivocal, and this equivocation (and the frequent failure to identify explicitly the meaning intended in a particular context) can be the cause of a great deal of intellectual mischief.

It can be a mistake to speak of *the* common good, as if there were one good (or collection of goods) that composed the common good.[57] Goods, or a good, may be said to be common in a number of ways. Most generally, however, we may say that a *common good* by definition is one that is, or may be, shared (owned, used, enjoyed, or pursued) by a number of persons.

Some goods are *naturally* common because they simply cannot be owned, used, or enjoyed by only one person at a time. Examples of natural common goods would include the view of a starry sky, the tradition and culture of a community, or knowledge of the natural law. Most goods, though, are *contingent* common goods; they may at some time be common but only because of a set of contingent factors that creates a context in which they are owned, used, or enjoyed by a number of persons. Examples of these goods would be wide-ranging but could include land, works of art, many kinds of knowledge, medicines, and money.

Goods are sometimes said to be common because their nature is such that they may be shared among an indefinite number of persons without diminishment. Knowledge is a good of this sort, as is a beautiful sunset. We can call these *infinite* common goods. By contrast, a *limited* or *finite* good is one that cannot be distributed to a number of persons (for their possession, use, or enjoyment) without diminishment. For example, a community of some kind may hold a supply

---

[57] We do, of course, speak of *the* common good as a sort of shorthand for the common good of a civil community. This is a legitimate usage, but it should not obscure for us the fact that there are many other important common goods.

of medicine in common. The supply of medicine is not owned by an individual or a limited group of people within the community but instead is the property of the community as a whole. (Of course, we could also be talking about land, money, food, housing space, or any other distributable resource.)

Both private goods and common goods may be actual or potential. *Actual* goods are those that, at a given point in time, really are owned, used, or enjoyed. *Potential* goods are those that, while not presently owned, used, or enjoyed, are viewed as possibly being so in the future. Actual goods do not, of course, motivate action intended to achieve them (because they are already possessed), though they may motivate protective action or action aimed at use or enjoyment. Potential goods, however, do serve to motivate goal-directed action, and potential common goods motivate collaborative action. Indeed, underlying any genuinely collaborative action (as opposed to an aggregate of individual actions aimed at the same goal, e.g., a gold rush), there must be at least one potential common good.

Potential common goods are frequently merely instruments for the attainment of private goods. Employees working together to make a company profitable may be less concerned about the long-term health and financial integrity of the business than about the things they may buy with the salary and bonus they receive from the successful operations of the firm. Such persons are not truly engaged in collaborative action but rather use a community of some sort to achieve their private goals. More thoughtful members recognize that, in addition to whatever private goals may be served by the effective operations of the association, there is also a goodness (associated with the good of friendship) to purposeful action pursued in communion with others. Action of this sort is more genuinely human, and such goal-directed action is defective when collaboration is avoided even though it might be effective.

Like other goods, common goods may also be *instrumental* or *final*. From the perspective of the individual, the potential common goods (i.e., common goals) toward which his or her actions are directed are always instrumental. That is, these common goods are valued by the individuals who pursue them in collaboration with others because they are always understood to promote private goods. Players work together on a team because each wants to be part of a winning effort, or at least each wants to share in the camaraderie of the group. Employees work toward the success of a business for similar reasons but also so that they can participate in the financial rewards.

On a larger scale, peace, order, and justice in a society are valued because they promote individual flourishing, not because they have an intrinsic value apart from their utility in supporting human well-being. Individuals may make extraordinary sacrifices to instantiate and protect such common goods, but it is because they understand and rightly value the private goods that follow.[58]

With respect to the actions of associations, though, common goods may have a kind of final character to the extent that the association ceases its collaborative activities once the good is attained. Thus, a committee may form to build a new playground for a community and disband once the playground is completed. The finished playground is a final good (goal) for the committee, even though the playground promotes (that is, is an instrument for) private goods (e.g.,

---

[58] Totalitarian states make the serious mistake of regarding such common goods as absolutely final and so in the end become willing to sacrifice all manner of private goods for their sake. Even in wiser societies, caution must always be exercised in crafting and applying positive laws so that the conditions that must exist in a society to promote the flourishing of its members are adequately protected while at the same time private goods are not threatened. To be sure, in any society, some private goods are incompatible with sustaining these public conditions and so may be legitimately curtailed—but a prudent balance must nevertheless be maintained.

health, play, friendships) indefinitely. Organizations that endure, such as businesses, churches, and the like, must either find new goals once the old ones are achieved or focus on goals that can only be sustained, never completed.

Potential common goods not only shape the collaboration of members of an organization, they also define organizations and communities. In particular, the potential common goods that define business organizations make them quite different from other kinds of communities.

Communities and Common Goods

Organizations are crucially important for modern life. Without organizations of the number, variety, and size that we see in the developed world, our quality of life simply could not be what it is. The incredible diversity of goods and services that we enjoy would not exist nor, in fact, would many other things that we have come to take for granted. Without smoothly functioning organizations, our diets would lose much of their variety; our health care would be much more primitive; and we would travel less, know less, and generally live poorer lives.[59]

Human beings are naturally inclined to form organizations, or more broadly communities, of all sorts, and for all sorts of reasons. The variety is limitless in one sense because we can always form communities for new and unprecedented purposes. In another sense, however, all communities fall into one of three categories.[60] In order to understand what an organization is (and what it is not) and to see

---

[59] There is no doubt that modern technologies and modern organizations have also served to introduce more stress into our lives and to coarsen them in a number of ways. This, however, is a result of our flawed use of technology and organizations, not an inevitable consequence of their mere existence.

[60] The criteria for categorizing communities have to do with the range of human goods they seek and the capabilities they possess, in principle, for achieving these goods.

what makes an organization excellent, it will be helpful to explore these three types and to see where organizations fall among them.

Aristotle was among the first to analyze human communities systematically. Where his teacher, Plato, speculated about the nature of the ideal state at length in his classic dialogue, *The Republic*, Aristotle set out to gather information about as many different cities and states as he could in order to understand communities as they really existed.[61]

He divided communities into three types, families, villages, and cities (or what today we might call *societies* or *political communities*), distinguished by function and in turn characterized by common goods peculiar to that form of community.[62] Families formed from the partnership of male and female, while villages, he argued, evolved naturally from groups of families and cities from villages.

On this analysis, the most inclusive community is a political community, or society. A political community can be understood in Aristotle's sense as one that makes available everything that is required for a truly good human life.[63] We might also call this a *complete* community.

The common good of a society has a distinctive character. Because societies are intended to endure over time and through successive generations, their characteristic common good does not consist in a goal to be achieved once and for

---

[61] Aristotle's principal treatise is the *Politics*. He also is reputed to have done an extensive study of the "constitutions" of a large number of Greek city-states. Only the *Constitution of Athens* has survived substantially intact, while the larger project exists only in fragments and quotations in other authors.

[62] See *Politics*, book 1.

[63] Aristotle did not assume that every political community necessarily possessed in fact all of the resources that would be required to fulfill its function. His point was rather that it is only in the political community that such resources could ever exist together and therefore that it is only in the political community that a truly full human life could be lived.

all. While there may be something potential about this common good, it is not a goal that, were it to be achieved, would mean the end of the society. Moreover, as the function of the society is to support the flourishing and fulfillment of its members, its common good is instrumental. That is to say, it is not a final good valued in and for itself (as basic goods are, for example), but it is something valued, supported, and protected by the members of the society for what it permits them to do and to be.

More precisely, the common good of a society is *constructive*, which means that it is a set of conditions that makes possible the individual flourishing of each and every member of the community.[64] To the extent that some necessary conditions are not present in a society, or that the well-being of some members is not addressed, the common good has not been achieved. We recognize as a practical matter that in a fallen world the set of goods and conditions that constitutes this common good is never fully achieved and so remains a goal for the members of the community. Even if it were to be achieved, the continued maintenance and support that it would require would still make it a goal entailing ongoing collaboration.

Another community is the family, and we might call this a *quasi complete* community. While the family clearly does not and cannot contain within itself all the resources necessary for a truly good human life, it is concerned with virtually every aspect of human flourishing, just as a political community is. Therefore, the common good of a family resembles the common good of a political community: It has as its goal every aspect of the flourishing of its members and so

---

[64] See Pope John XXIII, *Mater et magistra*, no. 65, for a classic definition of the common good of political communities. As a practical matter, this set of goods includes such elements as peace, justice, universal education, and participation in culture and public life.

requires peace, fairness, and so on. However, no family can supply by itself everything its members require; therefore, it may be more precise to say that its common good is to establish a set of conditions in which children can be raised to maturity (when they can take their places as responsible members of the political community), and the members can provide care and support to one another throughout their lives. Once again, this common good is instrumental and constructive, and so belongs in the same general category as the common good of a society.

A third kind of community—parallel with Aristotle's village—is a specialized association, or an *incomplete* community.[65] A specialized association, as the name implies, is ordered not to the integral fulfillment of its members but rather toward attaining some human good or limited set of goods. A business organization is a specialized association, as is an army, an orchestra, a charitable organization, a bowling club, a university, a criminal syndicate, and virtually an infinite number and variety of human organizations.

---

[65] As a subject of careful study, the city-state, or society, was Aristotle's particular focus. He devoted some attention to the family and the household (an anonymous essay on the subject was long thought to have been written by him) but not very much. Neither was he much interested in villages because he considered them to be a transitional group, a temporary development, wedged between the more enduring and important communities, family and society. Traditionally, when thinkers gave their attention to this alternate category, they tended to regard organizations either as overgrown families or as little societies. (How often have we heard, for example, about corporate "families" or organizational "politics"?) Today they deserve our attention in their own right. No doubt if Aristotle were alive today, he would have some interest in the nature of modern organizations and their role in social life. Until recently, following in Aristotle's footsteps, philosophers have tended to give emphasis to these political societies, and to a lesser degree to families, to the neglect of other associations. Therefore, while there has been over the centuries a great deal of ethical reflection on families and societies, there has been next to none on other groups.

Our understanding of the relationship between a specialized community and a political community needs further re-
finement. Until relatively recently (perhaps in some places
as late as the nineteenth century), specialized associations
played only a small role in human life.[66] In the twentieth century, however, that role has expanded greatly, both in terms
of the size of specialized associations and their numbers. In
developed societies today, virtually everyone is dependent
upon specialized associations, directly or indirectly.[67]

Specialized associations differ from political communities
and families in several important respects.

First of all, there is a difference in purpose. A specialized
association is always organized to pursue some particular
good or set of goods, at least for those who collaborate in the
association and often for others as well. Where the society or
family functions to sustain a set of conditions within which
persons may mature and seek their own fulfillment, a specialized association is directed to the creation of actual goods
that its members can possess.

---

[66] Some authors suggest that the triumph of the nation-state in Europe after
the seventeenth century dramatically diminished the role of what had been
a rich web of specialized associations (villages, churches, guilds, and so on).
In this earlier period, people tended to shape their personal identities from
their membership in these associations and therefore saw themselves as
integral and important parts of small wholes. After the seventeenth century,
people tended to see themselves as small parts of large wholes (i.e., nations).
While this may be so, it is also the case that these earlier specialized associations never achieved the size and extent of so many contemporary organizations.

[67] This is not to say, however, that we lead lives that are socially richer. In many
cases, while we may do what we do in the context of an organization of some
sort, we do these things not as members of a true human community but as
strangers in a crowd. Robert D. Putnam has described the curious decline of
community at a time of the increased importance of organizations in *Bowling
Alone: The Collapse and Revival of American Community* (New York: Simon &
Schuster, 2000).

Second, the nature of specialized associations makes their potential common goods (i.e., the goals of the organization) more important for their day-to-day functioning than would be the case in other communities. Goals shape collaboration. At the level of the family or the society, there is something natural about the collaboration of family members and citizens. Traditions and customs shape this collaboration, to be sure, but the ordinary citizen, for example, probably cooperates in supporting the common good of his community without much conscious thought.[68]

The same is not true of specialized associations. Here specific kinds of collaboration are required because of the organization's goals. To elicit this collaboration, the goals must be clearly understood, and they must be compelling. The success of the organization will require a certain kind of active contribution from each member, where the common good of a society can often be supported by the choices of citizens *not* to engage in behaviors that undermine this common good.

Third, specialized associations have both final and constructive common goods. The constructive common good, especially in a business organization, constitutes the conditions that must be maintained for the people in the business to do their work. These conditions include information, material resources, proper equipment, and so on. In addition, the conditions that are necessary to respect and enrich the personal dignity of the employees must be in place. The

---

[68] Of course, specific issues facing a society do often demand a great deal of deliberation and discussion, which is the function of legislative bodies. There are particular goals for which society must act but, properly speaking, these all relate back to the common good. For example, there are some instances in which the common good must be protected from threats from enemies or criminals and others in which a defect in the common good must be remedied. In both cases, the political will to act must be rallied.

work itself cannot be physically overwhelming, it must be fairly compensated, it must be worth doing and, in general, it cannot be demeaning or harmful to the people engaged in it.

Finally, specialized associations have a clear relationship to the societies in which they exist and function. It is sometimes assumed that to be legitimate specialized associations must serve the common good of the society in all that they do. This is a misunderstanding.

As we have discussed, the common good of a society is oriented to the flourishing of all of its members. This flourishing, however, entails the flourishing of the organizations and associations formed by members of the society to seek and obtain particular goods. These associations gain their legitimacy from the authentic human goods they seek, not from their contribution to the general common good. Indeed, the general common good must create the circumstances in which these organizations can function.

As a result, in a good society, these organizations should have considerable freedom in identifying and pursuing goods, which, to the extent that they serve to focus and motivate collaboration, will genuinely be common goods for that organization.[69] To be morally legitimate, these common goods must be true human goods (and not merely apparent goods, such as revenge or pornography), and they must be pursued by morally sound means. (A criminal organization might pursue real goods but do so by immoral means.) Of course, the pursuit of these goods should not undermine the constructive common good of the larger human community. However, *insofar as the goods pursued really are human goods, it is not necessary that the goods of a specialized association intentionally and directly support the common good of the larger community*. They may quite legitimately do nothing more than

---

[69] See *Compendium*, no. 354.

facilitate the attainment of private goods by those associated with the organization.[70]

These private goods may include the direct satisfaction of a variety of human needs, as well as opportunities for good work. Also included, and not least in importance, is the creation of wealth.

Business and the Creation of Wealth

The Catholic social tradition, rooted as it is in Scripture and developed in many contexts over two millennia, is not a tradition of preserving *applications* but a tradition of adapting *principles* to concrete situations. Some applications of Christian convictions, no matter how passionate and sincere, may not be appropriate to modern times and circumstances. Nevertheless, there are perennial principles that must be respected.

The term *wealth* has a special meaning in the Christian tradition. Unlike the discipline of economics and colloquial usage, the tradition tends not to speak of wealth as an abstract concept. Instead, there are countless references to the wealthy as a group, or to the "rich man." Used in this way, wealth is generally understood to be an excess of resources—typically money but perhaps also land, food, and

---

[70] That is, while the common goods of smaller communities must ordinarily be subordinated to the common good of the larger community within which it exists, it is not the case that the common goods of smaller communities must always be directed to serve the common good of the larger community. To put it another way, the actions of smaller communities or associations must not be such as to undermine the common good of the larger communities of which they are a part, although their actions need not always aim deliberately to enhance that common good in particular ways in order to be morally sound. Business organizations, therefore, need not use their resources to address social problems in order to be morally worthy associations. They are morally worthy if they pursue authentic goods in ways that properly respect other private goods and the common good of the larger community.

anything else of common value. Such material wealth is contrasted with spiritual wealth, and the tradition sometimes recognizes that those who possess much material wealth may be spiritually poor, and vice versa.

There is a related concept that plays a more important role in the tradition. If wealth is understood to imply excess, *abundance* and *prosperity* suggest something slightly different. The person who possesses wealth is ordinarily portrayed as unjust and impious. The common assumption is that his wealth is obtained and possessed in opposition to the needs of the poor and perhaps directly at their expense. Abundance and prosperity, however, are more commonly seen as gifts of God and as characteristic of God's unlimited love for his creatures. The man who possesses wealth is not usually regarded as blessed, but the person or community who enjoys abundance or prosperity does so as a blessing from the Lord. Abundance and prosperity, then, are surely good conditions, and, just as surely, poverty is a condition that requires a remedy.

If wealth is understood as an excess of material goods, then it is not a legitimate ambition for a Christian, or for anyone else, for that matter. Even Plato and Aristotle discouraged the pursuit of wealth as a life's ambition on the grounds that money in particular is merely a tool, not an end. To pursue the possession of a tool without regard for the purpose of possessing it is foolish and futile.

By the same token, some of the reasons one might have for seeking wealth are themselves empty. One might seek wealth for the sake of security—protection against the vagaries of life. For the Christian, as observed before, this can easily come to replace confidence in Providence and to distract one from the unique vocation that God intends. One might also seek wealth as a means to pleasure and comfort or as a tool to obtain honor or power. None of these, however, is consistent with the supernatural destiny of the person, and, as the early Christians saw so clearly, each of these goals is ultimately distracting and deadly. The contemporary experience of the developed world is striking evidence of the limitless appetite the human person has for each of these goals as well as of their capacity to crowd out and extinguish spiritual goods.

Wealth, then, understood as an excessive or perhaps unlimited quantity of money or material goods, can never be a rational objective for a good business. The accumulation of wealth for the explicit purpose of concentrating resources to support the common good in major ways might be a noble ambition, though a very dangerous one.[71] Far better is the goal of achieving abundance for oneself and one's family, including prosperity for one's community. Implied in this is a level of possessions adequate for one's genuine needs and security.

In the modern economy, many individuals accumulate more than this definition of abundance implies. The Christian social tradition, working from the principle that the goods of the earth are intended for all, has dealt with this

---

[71] It is easy to be reminded of Andrew Carnegie's famous essay, "The Gospel of Wealth" (*North American Review*, June 1889), in which he offers a sort of apologia for his life and the lives of others who have amassed great fortunes. He exhorts these men to use their wealth and power for the sake of the common good and urges the community to permit them to dispose of their wealth as they see fit. The very abilities that allowed them to acquire this wealth, he argues, make them the best suited to put it to use. Furthermore, the concentration of wealth in the hands of a few makes possible magnificent efforts that would be impossible if wealth were widely distributed (and so diluted). However, one can hardly fail to observe that such wealth is rarely accumulated by just men and thus rarely employed for the common good by men unaffected by injustice, vanity, power, and so forth. In keeping with the wisdom tradition in Scripture, the Christian view affirms that good men can be wealthy but they and others should understand that their wealth is a consequence of God's favor, not merely their own excellence. Such men do not cling to their wealth, as the wicked do, trusting in it to protect them from evil, but use it generously to relieve the widow, the orphan, and the stranger.

fact by insisting that such "surplus" wealth be used in ways that contribute to the extension of prosperity to all. Pope Pius XI provided a concrete example of the character of this obligation. In the midst of worldwide economic depression, he wrote, "Expending larger incomes so that opportunity for gainful work may be abundant" should be considered "an outstanding exemplification of the virtue of munificence and one particularly suited to the needs of the times."[72] Investing in employment-creating enterprise is one way to fulfill the obligations attending surplus wealth.

This abundance, bounded as it is by a clear focus on authentic human development and fulfillment, is certainly an ambition to be pursued by Christians. It is a blessing and an integral element of the common good of a political community. The Christian virtue of solidarity aims precisely at establishing such abundance and prosperity in every human community.

Abundance and prosperity are genuinely good conditions and worthy of pursuit, but how are they to be achieved? For much of Christian history, people tended to regard material goods, and the wealth they represented, as bounded in a strict sense. In other words, the quantity of wealth in the world was more or less fixed, and if some were quite wealthy (in the excessive sense), this could only be so at the expense of the poor. Thus, the problem of how to create prosperity in the community was viewed as essentially a problem of distribution.

More recently, it has become clear that the capacity of creation to serve genuine human needs, though perhaps finite in some sense, is practically limitless. This is not to say naively that the quantity of natural resources is so great that we cannot imagine exhausting it, but rather that human persons, in collaboration with the Creator, possess a capacity to *create* wealth, not merely to consume it. Creating wealth

---

[72] *Quadragesimo Anno*, no. 51.

means bringing increased order to creation and employing human intelligence and ingenuity to unlock nature's secrets and devise new ways to satisfy human needs. It means using new tools to make the earth productive, from growing more and better crops, to employing new forms of energy, to squeezing greater efficiencies from all sorts of activities. It means sharing technologies and techniques—among individuals and among nations—so that more and more people can participate in bringing about their own prosperity and that of their communities. It means, above all, using intelligence and knowledge to address real human needs, as understood within the context of an authentic anthropology and vision of human development.

The possibilities for this activity, released as it is from simple bondage to land or any other finite resource, are truly boundless.[73] It is a solemn Christian obligation, where possible, to seek not merely to distribute abundance but also to create it.

We are poised at the beginning of a new millennium but perhaps also at a set of other new beginnings as well. Catholics were strenuously encouraged by popes and bishops in the later half of the twentieth century to pay serious attention to the problems of poverty and inequity that characterize the human community. These problems persist and still deserve our attention whether we are members of developed communities or communities yet to develop fully. The world little needs more wealthy men and women; what it does need are more men and women who can create abundance and prosperity. This is preeminently, if not uniquely, the function of good businesses.

---

[73] See *Centesimus annus*, no. 32. Pope John Paul II clearly sees that human knowledge and skill are resources distinct in kind from land and capital and, as such, present possibilities for human prosperity and fulfillment that also differ in kind.

VI What Is the Good That Business Does?

We may now return to the question with which we began this book: What is the good that business does? How ironic that in the contemporary developed world, a world that enjoys a level of general prosperity unprecedented in human history, the answer to such a question is not obvious. Worse yet, not only is the good that business does often unappreciated, business is often cited as the cause of grave evils.

It may well be true that individual businesses sometimes act very badly and contribute in important ways to the world's evil and misery. Business is no more immune to corruption and misbehavior than is government, the church, the military, or any other human institution. The mere fact that businesses are populated and managed by fallible human beings who occasionally succumb to pressures and temptations should not blind us to the good that most businesses do. Having said this, however, our goal is not to explore the failures of businesses but rather to clarify what a good business is in addition to the good that business does.

What Is a Good Business?

In light of what we have already discussed, we can say now that a *morally* good business is one that attends to the goods proper to it as a specialized association and that employs ethically sound means to achieve these goods.[74] A business, like other specialized associations, is not legitimated by the contribution it makes to the common good of the civic community—though it must not act in ways that diminish this common good. It is instead made legitimate by the private goods that its activities make possible for its members and customers. The specific goods proper to a business will vary, of course, with the nature of the business, but we can identify in general the sorts of goods that businesses will need to pursue. These goods will include both common goods internal to the organization as well as private goods sought by individuals (employees, customers, and other collaborators) through their interaction with the business.

We should recall that because a business is a specialized association, the potential common goods (i.e., the goals) that shape the cooperative action of the members of the organization are focused upon specific private goods. That is, the ultimate purpose of a business will be to achieve some concrete goods for particular people. This is in contrast with families and civic communities where the potential common good is the comprehensive well-being of the members as human persons. Businesses, in other words, aim at the satisfaction of particular human needs, not at the entire ensemble of goods that make up a fully satisfactory human life.

---

[74] We can speak about *good* businesses in different ways, as when we say that a profitable enterprise is a good business or that a well-managed company is a good business. In the discussion here, however, we mean *good* in the deepest sense. A *good* business is one whose activities truly serve human needs in every important respect.

One of the characteristics of a *good* business, then, is that the goals of the organization are indeed directed to the satisfaction, directly or indirectly, of authentic human needs.[75] As we have discussed, such human needs are not necessarily desired by every person or even desired in the same form by every person. Nevertheless, a business that is not aimed at an authentic human good cannot, by definition, be a *good* business.

Businesses can go wrong in this regard by producing goods or services that respond merely to human wants but not needs.[76] Extreme examples would include pornography and nontherapeutic drugs, but more modest examples could be food products of no nutritional value or luxury items made exceptionally expensive by characteristics that add neither utility nor beauty.[77]

Most businesses avoid seriously bad products and services but too many are content to produce frivolous things instead of exercising their ingenuity to find new ways to address real needs. While this can be profitable in the short run, it cannot be the foundation of a sound and successful business. A truly good business requires the dedication of employees both to achieve excellence in what is produced and to cope

---

[75] Some businesses generate the products and services that immediately address the needs of end users. Others produce raw materials or supporting services that make it possible for the first sort of business to satisfy genuine human needs.

[76] Recall that a need is defined as something that genuinely contributes to human fulfillment. We sometimes want things that are not good for us to have, and businesses can sometimes exploit the willingness of customers to pay for products or services that, in the end, do them harm.

[77] "Gilding a lily" is an apt metaphor here. Some products or services may be luxurious in the sense that only a few people can afford them, but, in another sense, things can be luxurious when there is no value added to them beyond, say, the implication of status. For example, clothing differentiated only by the label and not by design or durability, might well fall into this category.

with the inevitable obstacles and setbacks. Employees cannot long dedicate themselves to producing trivial products and services (though they can go through the motions), and so a business will inevitably become mediocre (or worse) unless it focuses on real human needs.

A good business must also attend to the constructive common goods that shape an organization. These goods have to do with the conditions under which the organization conducts its activities and are analogous to the common good of a civic community. A good business is one in which these conditions are established and sustained. In general, they would include the rudiments of good management, such as clear communication; consistent and reasonable policies; safe working conditions; and a widely accepted culture in which fairness, honesty, and respect for persons are valued and expected. Management, of course, has a primary responsibility for creating and sustaining such a culture, but this responsibility is shared with every member of the organization. Because this is a common good, all members of the organization have both a duty to sustain its sound aspects by their behavior and a duty to avoid behaviors that would have the effect of undermining it. In sum, a good business is a good place to work.

These common goods, both potential and constructive, make possible the real contribution of business organizations, which is the achievement of specific private goods by and for a determinate group of people. These people are the members of the association and the customers. We can consider each group briefly in turn by considering why they associate or interact with the business.

In principle, the members of a specialized association are those who seek to achieve certain private goods through their voluntary participation in the activities of the organization. In the case of a business, the principal members are employees and owners or shareholders.[78] Each group seeks a distinct set of private goods.

It is not surprising that employees pursue the most varied set of goods. In the first place, of course, employees aim to earn a living through their participation in the organization's activities. Therefore, a good business makes the work of its employees genuinely productive, which is to say that their labor is coordinated, effective, and ordered to products and services that customers want to buy. As a result a stable income stream is created that would be proportionately greater than anything an individual employee would be able to create on his or her own. In turn, the employees should receive a fair share of this income stream.[79]

As Pope John Paul II has pointed out, however, people are motivated to work for reasons other than the income they hope to receive.[80] Employees also seek to express themselves

---

[78] A long discussion can be had about the status of shareholders, but we will set that question aside. The distinction that is important here is that employees participate in the business through the contribution of their work while owners and shareholders contribute property or money. Our discussion is not affected by the fact that employees can also be owners because, in such a case, they are seeking not one but two sets of private goods through their participation.

[79] In the Catholic social tradition, this fair share of the business's income must be no less than the practical minimum required to live a decent human life in the local community. This would include sufficient income to provide a reasonable standard of life for the employee's family: housing, clothing, food, health care, education, and so on. The tradition insists that this level of income belongs to the worker by right. It also insists, however, that the right is actualized through the labor of those able to work. Managers of a business, for their part, have a duty to pay a fair wage but also a duty to structure work in such a way that the contribution made by the average worker justifies the wage he needs.

[80] See Pope John Paul II, *Laborem exercens* ("On Human Work"), especially paragraph 9: "Work is a good thing for man—a good thing for his humanity—because through work man not only transforms nature, adapting it to his own needs, but he also achieves fulfillment as a human being and indeed in a sense becomes 'more a human being.'" A good business makes it possible for the employees to do just this.

through their work and to achieve something worthwhile. In a good business this "good work" becomes possible when employees can understand clearly what goods the organization's activities achieve and how their own work contributes to this good. Even work that is objectively unpleasant, tedious, or painful can be good work if its purpose can be known and appreciated.[81]

Employees are not merely an additional factor of production to be managed as efficiently as possible, but instead they are voluntary cooperators in the enterprise. As such, their dignity as persons must be respected, for example, in the way in which jobs are designed.[82] As free persons, it is appropriate that workers be permitted to exercise some freedom in the way in which they do their jobs and that they receive enough information about what they do to understand how their work contributes to a worthwhile goal.

Finally, a good business becomes a kind of *community* of work, in which persons freely collaborate to produce mutually satisfactory outcomes. One of these satisfactory outcomes is the friendship and socialization created by collaboration. People work in associations not simply because it is efficient to do so (though it may not always be efficient) but also because they are social creatures. It is neither natural nor personally rewarding for people to work in isolation. Indeed, one of the benefits of organizational work, one of the goods directly enjoyed by the employees, is friendship. Not every organization provides the same level of opportunity to form friendships, and not everyone in an organization will be open to friendships to the same degree. Nevertheless, friendships are important and often lie behind individual

---

[81] Parents of infants know that there are many tasks involved in caring for a baby that, however objectively unpleasant they may be, can nevertheless be good work because of the purpose they serve.

[82] John Paul reminds us, "in the final analysis it is always man who is the purpose of the work, whatever work it is that is done by man" (*Laborem exercens*, no. 6).

decisions to remain employed by a business, for example, even if pay and other working conditions are unsatisfactory.

With respect to the employees, then, a good business provides an opportunity to earn a fair and satisfactory income, to be engaged in good work, and to form rewarding friendships.

The goods sought by owners and shareholders are less varied. The principal private good that they seek is a return on their investment, ordinarily in the form of a cash dividend or a cash profit on the sale of stock. This cash, of course, is an instrumental good, not a good in itself, but a good business need not be concerned with the uses to which its investors put their profits. The objective of the good business in this regard is merely to create wealth for the investors in a manner consistent with all other moral and legal obligations.[83]

Investors, however, have one additional relevant objective. They have a moral obligation to use their property well, and a good business provides them with an opportunity to do just that. This is not to say that investing in a business is the best use of cash or other assets; that determination depends on particular contexts. All we need to say is that investing in a good business can be a morally sound use of property, and a good business will consistently provide such an opportunity because it is directed to the satisfaction of real human needs. In providing that opportunity, it furnishes a private good for investors.

---

[83] We will set aside a discussion of the question of whether a business ought to seek to maximize shareholder wealth. Suffice it to say that if this is understood to mean that a good business must give priority to the creation of wealth for shareholders over the other goods it properly seeks, then a good business cannot aim at maximization. Other goods, such as the safety of employees or the preservation of their jobs, may at times deserve a higher priority. On the contrary, if a business seeks to create as much wealth as it can consistent with its obligations and the other goods it seeks, then maximization is an appropriate goal.

The third group for whom a good business provides private goods is customers. These private goods, of course, are served by the products and services provided by the business. We have observed at length that these products and services must address genuine human needs, but this constitutes a kind of moral minimum. No business can be truly good if it does not satisfy this criterion, but to be excellent it must do more.

First, the products and services of an excellent business will serve human needs especially well. They will be well designed and well made or executed. Second, they will be offered to customers at a good and fair price.[84] This often means that excellent businesses will find ways to improve efficiency and eliminate waste. Third, excellent businesses offer products and services that are safe for customers to use under circumstances that can be reasonably foreseen. No business can be responsible for all misuses or abuses of its products. It can, and should, however, take steps to limit harms that may arise from foreseeable abuses.[85]

To sum up, then, a good business must meet several criteria because there are several proper goods that it should seek simultaneously. It should have worthwhile goals and establish conditions of operation that fully respect human dignity. It should permit employees to earn a living and give them good work to do. It should put the resources of owners and shareholders to good use and create wealth for them. Finally, it must actually offer to customers products and services that satisfy genuine human needs at fair prices. The list may

---

[84] A considerable literature exists on the subject of fair price. (See, for example, James Gordley, "Equality in Exchange." *California Law Review* 69 [1981]: 1587–1656.) In principle, a fair price is determined by a market that functions properly. A good company does not use market shortcomings or deliberate techniques to extract an unfairly high price from its customers.

[85] For example, manufacturers of firearms should continue to seek ways to diminish the possibility of harm from misuse of weapons. These means could include better safety mechanisms, more aggressive training, and so on.

seem daunting when it is broken down like this but a moment's thought should confirm that many businesses do in fact aim at much the same set of goals. For our purposes, the critical point is not whether these goals are difficult to accomplish or whether few or many businesses succeed in achieving them. The critical point is that nothing more is required to make a business morally legitimate; if a business is doing these things, its place in society is justified.

The Contribution of Business to the Common Good

Newly emerged in the modern world is a sophisticated commercial system that makes possible the creation and distribution of products and services on an unprecedented scale. Even though a business need not make a direct contribution to the common good of the civic community in order to be good and legitimate, business as a system does make such contributions. The system organizes and integrates a number of separate elements for the sake of the common good. These elements include:

1. A business culture in which individual businesses, from small to large, create an environment in which certain procedures and values are shared for the sake of more effective collaboration and even competition;[86]

---

[86] Despite some dramatic exceptions, contemporary business relationships and operations are facilitated by a culture in which certain attitudes and practices are taken for granted. These include respect for market mechanisms, an attitude of service, and commitments in practice to transparency and good record keeping, honoring promises, and so on. By way of illustration, as formerly Communist countries worked to reenter a global marketplace in the 1990s, one of the things businesspeople were particularly keen to learn from the West was the set of habits required to compete and be taken seriously.

2. A stable financial infrastructure, which depends on sound fiscal and monetary policies and international cooperation;
3. A system of laws and regulations concerning business operations that are stable, economically sound, and ordered to the common good;
4. The effective application of technology, especially in the areas of communication and transportation, that serves to facilitate business operations.

The history of the development of modern business need not concern us here. It is sufficient to say that the invention and spread of the limited liability corporation made possible the creation of the large organizations required for many modern products and services.[87] These organizations could survive their founders, and the principle of limited liability encouraged investors to take risks. The early successes of these organizations gave some indication of the possibilities (and the perils) that lay ahead. Over time, we came to realize that exploiting the potential of this new way of doing business would also require the cooperation of government in setting in place sound financial policies as well as sensible laws and regulations. It was also necessary for government to take a hand in shaping the development and use of new technologies that would facilitate business operations (among other things), from railroads, interstate highways, and air travel, to the Internet and modern telecommunications.

---

[87] Many of the foundations of modern life would be impossible without large business organizations. From railroads, automobiles, and aircraft to telecommunications, computers, and modern medicine, much of what we take for granted cannot be produced entirely by small companies. The limited liability corporation made practical the assembly of financial resources required by these large businesses.

Much of the government interest in the development of the modern business system was motivated, or at least justified in public discussion, by a concern for the common good of the community. When it functions well, the modern system of business contributes to that common good chiefly in two ways.[88]

First, the system of business augments the wealth-producing capacity of the community. In the Christian tradition, wealth is not understood simply as money but rather as an abundance of the material goods required for a good human life. To create wealth is to apply human labor and ingenuity to the resources of creation in order to produce the goods that satisfy human needs. To have an abundance of these goods is to be prosperous, and, in the most important sense (because human persons are social creatures), prosperity is a sought-after condition of communities and societies, not merely individuals. The wealth-producing capacity of a society, therefore, is its ability to bring into being the abundance or prosperity necessary to sustain the good life for each of its members.[89]

---

[88] Like any powerful tool, this system can be abused and turned against the common good. This fact should not be ignored, but neither should we make business the natural enemy of society and overlook the real good it is capable of doing.

[89] One might argue that this abundance of goods is impossible to achieve because human wants are unlimited; as soon as one desire is satisfied another one can arise. However, a truly good life for an individual is not the satisfaction of every desire but rather the reasonable satisfaction of the desires of a virtuous person. The deepest human desires, the ones that are properly unlimited, are spiritual and intellectual, not material. Therefore, it remains possible in principle to generate an abundance of goods. That even "wealthy" societies fail to do this may say more about the reasonableness of their desires than about the capacity of the society to create prosperity. Furthermore, as a practical matter, unlimited goods would require unlimited productive labor. While a good life requires some good work, it also requires leisure properly understood. Therefore, in a prosperous society, material goods are available in abundance, thus making a good life possible, but desires are moderated by virtue as well, thus making unlimited goods unnecessary.

Business does this in two ways. In the first place, it organizes human work more effectively, making the worker more productive without necessarily demanding more time and energy from him.[90] Second, business in many societies has the task of converting common resources (whether natural, such as oil, or virtual, such as bandwidth) into useful products and services.[91] Participants in developed economies generally recognize that business manages this conversion better than the public sector and therefore contributes more to the common good by doing so. Thus, in more highly developed economies, many activities are privatized that once were conducted by a branch of government.

Now, business does not have a monopoly, so to speak, on productive human labor. Wealth can be created by any segment of society, but business by its nature focuses on wealth-creating activities. Well-managed business, of whatever size, while they aim at particular goods for their members and customers, also augment the capacity of a society to create general prosperity, which is indeed an element of the common good. To put it another way, no society in our experience has ever achieved a significant level of prosperity without a healthy and robust business sector.

The second broad contribution to the common good that the system of business makes is related to the first. Business organizes work and resources to generate not only *more* products and services to address the material needs of members of the community but also better and more sophisticated ones.

---

[90] Needless to say, businesses are not immune to the disorganization and inefficiency that are found in other sectors. However, incentives to deal with these problems are more strongly present in business settings than in most nonprofit or government organizations. Very few people, if any, recommend that businesses study government agencies or university faculties to find models of efficiency and effectiveness.

[91] That is, societies convey to businesses in some fashion the right to extract or exploit a resource owned by the community. In doing so, the society may benefit from a fee paid to acquire the rights as well as from the relatively efficient conversion of the resource into something that serves human welfare.

The Social Responsibility of Business

In 1946, Congress enacted changes in the tax code that permitted publicly held business corporations to deduct charitable donations in amounts up to 5 percent of their federal taxable income. Congress, of course, did not require companies to make charitable donations, but it did encourage them to do so. The legislation became one more landmark in a running controversy about corporate social responsibility.

Simply put, this controversy concerns the question of whether publicly held business corporations (sole proprietorships and partnerships must be treated somewhat differently) have a duty to the communities in which they operate that goes beyond the duty to obey the law in the conduct of their operations. If they have such a duty, questions remain about why they have that duty and what exactly it requires them to do.

By contrast, the attention given to the study of business ethics over the last several decades has served to reinforce the conviction that business corporations have a social responsibility that *requires* them to use some of their resources to address needs in their communities. These resources may be cash, or physical property, or even the time and energy of their employees. Ordinarily, the needs addressed are outside the scope of the normal operations of the company. As a result, corporations make significant contributions to the arts or to social service organizations. In doing this, advocates argue, they are merely being good corporate citizens and giving something back to the society. We may call this the *strong view* of corporate social responsibility.

Many opponents of this view insist that business corporations have no responsibility to society beyond obeying the law as they go about their operations. Their principal and overriding responsibility is to shareholders, and it is a responsibility to conduct the operations of the company in such a way as to maximize the wealth of these shareholders.

We may call this the *weak view* of corporate social responsibility. Perhaps the best known proponent of the weak view is Milton Friedman, the Nobel laureate in economics.[92]

Over the last decade or two, as some version of the strong view has become the common opinion in business schools and executive suites, thinking about the nature of the business corporation and its relationship to the community has also changed. Quite often the moral quality of a company has been evaluated in terms of its commitment to social responsibility. In practice, however, this has created at least two kinds of problems, which on occasion have been serious and that, in any event, should provoke us to reconsider the wisdom and soundness of the strong view of corporate social responsibility.

The first kind of problem is that the specific nature of corporate contributions sometimes becomes an obstacle to the successful conduct of business. Several companies have received unwelcome publicity and have been the target of customer outrage because of their support for or opposition to controversial social programs. A few years ago, for example, Berkshire-Hathaway decided to curtail its corporate giving after customers of one of its companies objected to Warren Buffett's own generous support of population control activities. More generally, socially responsible investment funds often screen stocks by examining the company's cor-

---

[92] Friedman wrote an article for the *New York Times Magazine* (30 September 1970) in which he argued that business corporations best serve their societies when they increase their profitability. Executives of business corporations, he said, had no warrant to use the assets of the company for charitable purposes. To do so would constitute, in his judgment, an illicit tax on the shareholders because it would be a use of their money for public purposes that was neither lawfully required nor consensual. Friedman's argument in this article is sometimes interpreted to mean that businesses have no obligations beyond what they assume voluntarily and what are imposed by law. In fact, in this same article, he acknowledged that businesses are also bound by the "basic rules of society ... embodied in ethical custom."

porate giving. As these funds have become larger and more numerous, their impact on corporate giving practices is likely to be felt. In many cases, a contribution approved by one fund will cause another fund to reject the investment.

A second sort of problem is more subtle, but its effects have been displayed quite dramatically over the last two years. There can be a dark side to corporate philanthropy, as companies such as Enron have demonstrated. Enron conducted a very generous corporate giving program, and this tended to make people reluctant to examine the company's business practices too closely. In Enron's case, a member of the audit committee of the board was also a faculty member at a university that was a grateful beneficiary of the company's largesse. In other cases, corporate donations have funded projects directed by the spouses of members of Congress or other officials. Even where there are less egregious conflicts of interest, nonprofit organizations and the people who benefit from their services can bring influence to bear to support their donors over against the community as a whole (as for instance when artificial barriers prevent competitors from entering a marketplace). A related problem arises when such corporation-sponsored organizations, through political or intellectual activity, seek to undermine the market system itself, thereby making more difficult the extension of prosperity to an ever larger number of beneficiaries. For these reasons, we need to ask whether the strong view of corporate social responsibility is well-grounded in a proper understanding of the nature of a business corporation and whether it is an accurate description of whatever social responsibility it may have.

The relative newness of the corporate form has caused us to puzzle about its nature. The law, for example, regards it as if it were a person for some purposes and as if it were an object of ownership for other purposes (while at the same time insisting that "persons" cannot be owned). In still other contexts, the law considers corporations not so much to be things as to be networks of contractual relationships. Nevertheless, in each of these instances the determining principle behind the relevant legal concept of the corporation is rooted not in some conclusion about the nature of the corporation but rather in a problem the law wishes to resolve. Treating the corporation as if it were a person or an object of ownership or a network of contracts allows the courts to resolve the problem at hand, but we should not be misled by this into thinking that the law has told us what a corporation truly is.

Ethicists, economists, and social scientists each similarly grasp an important piece of the whole, relevant to their own disciplines, without necessarily accurately describing the whole. Thus, for ethicists, the corporation is (or perhaps is not) a moral agent; for economists, it is a set of relationships designed to optimize efficiency; and for social scientists it is a social arrangement with its own culture, both like and unlike families and civil societies.

As we have discussed, business corporations enhance the common good by providing good employment, by producing needed goods and services, and by creating wealth. Their potential to do this is so great, in fact, that the prosperity of a modern society can be directly correlated with the presence in the society of this corporate structure. In principle, therefore, the community permits and protects this form of association because it makes a particularly important contribution to the common good when it functions properly. Additionally, the community retains the right to regulate corporations in order to insure as far as possible that it does function properly and that it does make this contribution.

Business corporations, therefore, by their nature serve the common good when they function as they should. They are not grudging concessions made by society to the greed of executives and investors. As a result, the primary social responsibility of a business corporation is, in fact, to make the contribution to the common good that it is uniquely structured to make. It need not justify its existence on the ground that it addresses broad social injustices or performs general works of charity.

Yet, the rationale sometimes offered for the strong view of corporate social responsibility implies that producing economic benefits is not enough; business corporations must do more. Insisting, for example, that businesses must "give something back to the community" suggests both that they are not adequately contributing to the common good through their normal operations (which include paying taxes) and that their operations unfairly take something away from the community. Neither suggestion bears close examination.

When business corporations are created, the community does not give something away. Instead, in order to pursue the economic benefits offered by the corporate structure, the community offers something in exchange. It offers to recognize the corporation as a stable, enduring entity and to limit the civil liability of its members (i.e., its employees and investors). Any fair assessment of the impact of the corporate structure on communities would conclude that the communities sacrifice little and gain much. (Indeed, one might also fairly ask whether the exchange a community makes in sacrificing tax revenues in order to support nonprofit corporations creates proportional benefits for the common good.)

This does not mean that business corporations have no corporate social responsibility beyond conducting their operations within the law. Where the strong view of corporate social responsibility demands too much, the weak view (that corporations need only obey the law) requires too little. Law by its very nature is reactive; laws and regulations are enacted to prevent harms we have experienced in the past from occurring again. They rarely, if ever, anticipate harms we have never experienced and offer proactive protection. As a result, the law constitutes a minimal set of requirements for ethically sound behavior for individuals and organizations.

(That we sometimes think laws or regulations become too detailed in their prescriptions is a different matter.)[93]

Corporations, in other words, like morally upright individuals, have responsibilities that are not adequately described by laws and regulations. These genuine corporate social responsibilities concern both what they ought to do and what they ought to avoid.

On the positive side, corporations have a duty to treat their major constituencies as fairly as they can. They should also be ready to address needs in their fields of operation that are not well served and may not be very profitable. For example, grocery wholesalers and retailers could be open to ways in which they could help to insure that no one in the community goes hungry; construction companies could explore ways in which affordable housing could be built; and pharmaceutical companies could propose creative and effective partnerships with government to make medications available more cheaply.

Concerning what they ought to avoid, business corporations have a responsibility to avoid causing harms to the community (e.g., pollution) even when those harms are not prohibited by law. They have similar duties not to exploit employees or manipulate customers, regardless of whether the specific sorts of exploitation or manipulation are subject to regulation. They also have a duty not to use their economic and political power to secure legislation that is unfairly favorable to them (such as artificial barriers to the entry of competitors to the market).

---

[93] There is the danger of legal overreaction, for example, when genuine corporate wrongdoing (as in the case of Enron, and so forth) stimulates overly burdensome regulatory legislation that, while intended well, serves less to encourage moral behavior than to make more difficult the fulfillment of businesses' legitimate ends.

These examples do not exhaust the possibilities for discharging the responsibilities of business corporations to their communities, but they do illustrate the direction in which these responsibilities run.

Nor do these limits mean that business corporations should not donate money or other assets to the community. Business corporations are at liberty to make whatever donations they wish to address and whatever needs they choose. The key, of course, is the difference between obligation and freedom. What is not required may still be permitted. In the case of business corporations, donations may be made when doing so will not undermine the legitimate operations of the business, when employees and customers will not be harmed, and when shareholders consent.

Corporate philanthropy has accomplished much good. No doubt it should continue vigorously—but not at the expense of a company's more fundamental and important social responsibilities: to create wealth, to provide good jobs, and to offer products and services that serve genuine human needs. These are the principal objectives of businesses as specialized associations, and it is in these areas that we recognize the tremendous good that business does.

References

Church Documents

Compendium of the Social Doctrine of the Church. Vatican City: Libreria Editrice Vaticana, 2004.

Pope Pius XI. Encyclical Letter *Quadragesimo Anno.* 1931.

Pope John XXIII. Encyclical Letter *Mater et magistra.* 1961.

Pope John Paul II. Encyclical Letter *Centesimus annus.* 1991.

Pope John Paul II. Apostolic Exhortation *The Vocation and Mission of the Lay Faithful (Christifideles laici).* 1988.

Pope John Paul II. Encyclical Letter *Sollicitudo rei socialis.* 1987.

Pope John Paul II. Encyclical Letter *Laborem exercens.* 1981.

Documents of the Second Vatican Council:
Dogmatic Constitution on the Church (Lumen gentium)
Pastoral Constitution on the Church in the Modern World
   (Gaudium et spes)
Decree on the Apostolate of the Laity (Apostolicam actuositatem).

Books and Articles

Aristotle. *Politics.*

Avila, Charles. *Ownership: Early Christian Teaching.* Maryknoll, N.Y.: Orbis Books, 1983.

Bainbridge, Steven. "Law and Economics: An Apologia." In *Christian Perspectives on Legal Thought*, ed. Michael McConnell, Robert G. Cochran, Jr., and Angela Carmella. New Haven, Conn.: Yale University Press, 2001.

Carnegie, Andrew. "The Gospel of Wealth." *North American Review* 148 (June 1889): 653–54.

Chafuen, Alejandro A. *Faith and Liberty: The Economic Thought of the Late Scholastics*. Lanham, Md.: Lexington Books, 2003.

Finley, M. I. *The Ancient Economy*. Berkeley: University of California Press, 1973.

Finnis, John. *Natural Law and Natural Rights*. Oxford: Oxford University Press, 1980.

Friedman, Milton. "The Social Responsibility of Business Is to Increase Its Profits." *New York Times Magazine*, 30 September 1970.

Gordley, James. "Equality in Exchange." *California Law Review* 69 (1981): 1587–1656.

Grabill, Stephen J. et al. *Doing Justice to Justice*. Grand Rapids, Mich.: Acton Institute, 2002.

Grice-Hutchinson, Marjorie. *Early Economic Thought in Spain*. Boston: G. Allen and Unwin, 1978.

Grisez, Germain. *The Way of the Lord Jesus*. Vol. 1, *Christian Moral Principles*. Chicago: Franciscan Herald Press, 1983.

Michel, Humfrey. *The Economics of Ancient Greece*. New York: Macmillan, 1940.

Noonan, John T. *The Scholastic Analysis of Usury*. Cambridge, Mass: Harvard University Press, 1957.

Novak, Michael. *The Spirit of Democratic Capitalism*. New York: Simon & Schuster, 1982.

Phan, Peter C. *Social Thought*. Message of the Fathers of the Church, no. 20. Wilmington, Del.: Michael Glazier, 1984.

Plato, *The Laws*.

Plato, *The Republic*.

Putnam, Robert D. *Bowling Alone: The Collapse and Revival of American Community*. New York: Simon & Schuster, 2000.

Schumpeter, Joseph. *The History of Economic Analysis*. New York: Oxford University Press, 1954.

Widow, Juan Antonio. "The Economic Teachings of Spanish Scholastics." In *Hispanic Philosophy in the Age of Discovery*, ed. Kevin White. Studies in Philosophy and the History of Philosophy, no. 29. Washington, D.C.: Catholic University of America Press, 1997.

About the Author

ROBERT G. KENNEDY is a full professor and chair of the Department of Catholic Studies at the University of St. Thomas (St. Paul, Minnesota) and co-director of the University's Terrence J. Murphy Institute for Catholic Thought, Law, and Public Policy. He also holds a joint appointment in the College of Business, where he served as chair of the faculty in 2004–05. He received his Ph.D. in medieval studies with a concentration in philosophy and theology from the University of Notre Dame, and also holds master's degrees in biblical criticism and business administration. He is the author of some two hundred essays, book reviews, and articles on a variety of topics, including corporate social responsibility, professionalism, spirituality in the workplace, wealth creation, ethical investment, and other issues related to culture and public life.